Leonardo Boff was born in
doctorate from the University
For the following 20 years, he w̲ ̲
Franciscan School for Philosophy and Theology in Petropolis,
Brazil. During the 1970s, he and Gustavo Gutiérrez helped
to define Liberation Theology. Since 1993, he has been a pro-
fessor at the State University of Rio de Janeiro, where he is
now Emeritus Professor of Ethics, Philosophy of Religion and
Ecology. He is also a member of the International Earth
Charter Commission. Professor Boff is the author of more than
70 titles, including *Jesus Christ Liberator: A Critical Christology
for Our Time.* Owing to the views he expressed in his book
Church: Charisma and Power, he was investigated by the
Sacred Congregation for the Doctrine of the Faith in the
Vatican by Cardinal Ratzinger (now Pope Benedict XVI).
Fundamentalism, Terrorism and the Future of Humanity was
published by SPCK in 2006.

ESSENTIAL CARE

An Ethics of Human Nature

LEONARDO BOFF

Translation and notes
Alexandre Guilherme

First published in Great Britain in 2007

Society for Promoting Christian Knowledge
36 Causton Street
London SW1P 4ST

The author and publisher have made every effort to ensure that the
external website and email addresses included in this book are
correct and up to date at the time of going to press. The
author and publisher are not responsible for the content,
quality or continuing accessibility of the sites.

British Library Cataloguing-in-Publication Data
A catalogue record for this book is available from the British Library

ISBN 978–0–281–05853–5

1 3 5 7 9 10 8 6 4 2

Typeset by Graphicraft Limited, Hong Kong
Printed in Great Britain by Ashford Colour Press

Produced on paper from sustainable forests

To Marcia
whose example of care
inspired this book;
and who, through her support and collaboration,
became a true co-author of this book.

Contents

Note to reader

An asterisk in the text denotes a word that will be found in the Glossary.

Foreword – Tamagochi and care

Today's society, which is often called the society of knowledge and communication, is in contradiction increasingly creating more solitude in and miscommunication between people. The Internet can connect us to millions of people without the need to physically meet anyone. We can do our shopping, we can pay our bills, we can do our work, we can order food and we can watch a film without the need to speak to anyone. We can even go travelling; we can get to know countries and art galleries in extraordinary detail without the need to leave our homes. Everything is *online*; everything comes to our homes through our Internet connections.

Our relationship with concrete reality, with its smells, its colours, its sensations of heat and cold, its different weights and its diverse resistances and contradictions is mediated through the virtual image, which is solely image. Our feet no longer feel the softness of the green lawn, nor do our hands clutch a fistful of dark earth. The virtual world has created a new habitat for the human being, a habitat that is characterized by a cocooning of the human being and by the impossibility of touching, through its lack of tactile experiences and of human contact.

This anti-reality affects human life in what it possesses as most fundamental: care and compassion. Ancient myths and important contemporary thinkers teach us that the human essence is found not so much in intelligence, in freedom or in creativity but is rather found in care. Care is, in fact, the real support of creativity, freedom and intelligence. Care is the fundamental ethos* of the human being.[1] That is to say, in care we find the principles, the values, and the attitudes that turn life into good living and actions into righteous actions.

The kind of society based on knowledge and communications that we have developed in the past decades threatens the human essence. Has it not discarded the features of real people's faces, the shape of their hands, the liveliness of their presences, their personal histories moulded by their searches, challenges, bewilderments, failures and victories? Has it not cast doubt on, and even slandered as an obstacle to objective knowledge, the capacities to care, to be sensitive and to be moved? Are not these capacities really necessary and qualities without which nobody can survive and live meaningfully? Does this society not perhaps, to the extent that it advances technologically in the production and services of material goods, also produce more impoverished and excluded people, those almost two-thirds of human kind, who are condemned to die before their time?

My reflections here seek to denounce such deviation. I dare to present ways to cure and to rescue the human essence, ways that pass through care.

I nurture the profound conviction that care, by the fact that it is essential, can be neither suppressed nor discarded. It seeks revenge and always breaks through some of the breaches of life. I emphasize: if it were not like this, then it would not be essential. Where does care appear in our society? In something that is very common, in something that is almost ridiculous, but in something that is extremely suggestive: it appears in the tamagochi.

What is the tamagochi? It is a Japanese invention first seen in 1997. It is an electronic key ring with three buttons underneath its small liquid crystal screen, which a virtual pet inhabits. This small pet feels hunger, eats, sleeps, grows up, plays, cries, gets sick, and can even die. It depends on the care that it receives or does not receive from its owner.

The tamagochi requires a lot of work. Like a child it requires constant care and if it does not receive this care then it complains with a *bleep*; if it is not answered there are risks. Who is so heartless that they would leave a pet to die?

This toy has become a craze and it has changed the routine of many children, teenagers and adults who take the utmost care of their tamagochi, feed it, let it have a rest and let it go to sleep. Care can even perform the miracle of resurrecting it, should it have died for lack of attention and care.

An observant columnist in Rio de Janeiro noted well when he said: 'Solitude, its codename is tamagochi.' Caring for the virtual pet denounces the solitude in which the men and women of the emerging society of communication are living. It announces, however, that despite the dehumanization of a great part of our culture, the human essence has not been lost. The human essence is there in the form of care, which has been transferred into an electronic device and which is no longer invested in concrete people around us: in the sick grandmother, in a handicapped friend from school, in a street kid, in the old man who sells bread to us in the morning, in the poor and marginalized people of our cities, and even in a real pet, whatever kind of pet it be, a hamster, a parrot, a cat or a dog.

The issue of care serves as a critique of the agonizing situation of our civilization, but it also serves as an inspiring principle for a new paradigm of living together. This is what I propose to present in this book.

I dream of a world that is still to come, a world where we will no longer need electronic devices with virtual beings in order to overcome our solitude and fulfil the human essence of care and kindness. I dream of a globalized society, in the great common home of the Earth, where structuring values are built around caring for people, especially those who are culturally different, those who have been penalized by nature or by history; based on care for those who are needy and who have been excluded – the children, the elderly, the dying; based on care for plants, animals, landscapes that are dear to us, and especially care for our great and generous mother, the Earth. I dream of a world in which care has been recognized as a fundamental ethos of the human being and as an indispensable compassion for all the beings in creation.

1

Carelessness: a sign of our times

This book has been written as a matter of urgency. We see everywhere symptoms, signs of great devastations affecting the planet Earth and humankind. The project based on unlimited material growth, and which is globally integrated, sacrifices two-thirds of humanity, exhausts the natural resources of the Earth and compromises the future of generations to come. We now find ourselves at the crossroads of extraordinary new pathways. How much more can the supra-organism-Earth take? Are we heading towards a kind of chaotic civilization?

Throughout its existence the Earth has suffered unimaginable cataclysms, but it has always survived them. The Earth has always safeguarded the principles and the diversity of life.

We hope that it will not be different this time. There are chances of salvation, but for this to occur we must follow a long path, a path where we need to change our daily and political habits, our private and public lives and our cultural and spiritual practices. The increasing degradation of our common home, the Earth, is a sign of a crisis that has been brought about because of our immaturity. It is now important for us to enter our mature years and to show signs of our wisdom. If we do not do this then we cannot guarantee a promising future for ourselves.

Let us then formalize the problem here. It could be said: we are not experiencing the end of the world, we are in fact experiencing the end of a *type* of world. We are facing a crisis affecting human civilization. We are in need of a new paradigm for living together. Such a new paradigm will be based on better relations with the Earth, which will inaugurate a new social pact between peoples, a social pact forged in respect and for the preservation of all that exists and is alive. Only if these changes occur will it make sense for us to start thinking about alternatives that may present us with new hope.

Symptoms of a crisis in civilization

The most painful symptom, which has been acknowledged for a considerable period by respectable commentators and thinkers of our time, is a widespread indisposition affecting civilization. This indisposition manifests itself in the guise of neglect, of disregard and of abandonment; in short, it manifests itself as a lack of care.

There is an attitude of neglect and disregard for the lives of innocent children, who have been used as a power source for production aimed at the global market. A report in 1998 from UNICEF reveals some terrifying data: 250 million working children. In Latin America, three out of every five children are engaged in labour. In Africa, one in three children and in Asia, one in two children is engaged in labour. These children are small slaves to whom childhood, innocence and dreams have been denied. When these children are killed by death squads in the large cities of Latin America and Asia it no longer makes the news.

There is an attitude of neglect and disregard for the destiny of the poor and marginalized of humankind, who have been afflicted by harsh famines. They have barely survived the tribulations of many diseases, some of which had once been eradicated and which are now making a comeback with even greater virulence.

There is an attitude of neglect and disregard for the fate of the unemployed and retired; above all for the fate of those millions who have been excluded from a system of production that considers them disposable and economically unviable. These millions of excluded do not even have the privilege of being considered a labour reserve by the capitalist system; they have lost the privilege of being exploited at the price of a minimum wage and a few social benefits.

There is an attitude of neglect and abandonment of acts of kindness. These have been undermined by the current dominance of neoliberalism, with its individualism and its exaltation of private property. There is a disdainful attitude towards solidarity and a scornful attitude towards ideals of liberty and dignity for all human beings. This situation has worsened with the fall of true socialism and the implosion of the Soviet bloc. Despite the contradictions that were present in these, true socialism and the Soviet bloc always actively maintained the rhetoric of the social, and kept alight the conscience of cooperation and internationalism.

There is an attitude of neglect and a growing abandonment of sociability in cities. The majority of inhabitants feel culturally uprooted and socially alienated. There is a predominance of society based on spectacle, shallow appearances and entertainment.

There is an attitude of neglect and disregard for the spiritual aspect of the human being, for the *esprit de finesse*, the spirit of kindness that cultivates the logic of the heart and that brings about a feeling of awe for everything that exists and is alive. There is no caring attitude towards emotions, towards the imaginary and towards the angels and demons that inhabit it. All kinds of violence and excesses are shown by the means of communication, with a total lack of decency or scruples.

There is an attitude of neglect and disregard in public affairs. Poor policies are implemented in tackling poverty, and investments in social security for the provision of proper food, health, education and housing are in general inappropriate. There is a shameful attitude of neglect for the level of morality in public life, which is stained by corruption and by the explicit power struggle between groups, wallowing in the mire of corporate interests.

There is an abandonment of the attitude of reverence, and this attitude is extremely important if one is to care for life and for its fragility. If things continue as they are, at the beginning of the twenty-first century CE, more than half of the species of animals and plants that currently exist will certainly disappear. This has been acknowledged by a recent and highly regarded report on the state of the planet Earth published in the United States: *The State of the Environment Atlas*. The disappearance of these species represents the disappearance of a library of knowledge that has been accumulated by the universe during the course of 15 billion years of hard evolutionary work.

There is an attitude of neglect and disregard insofar as safe-guards for our common home, the planet Earth, are concerned. The soil is being poisoned, the air is being contaminated, the water is being polluted, forests are being decimated, species of living beings are being exterminated and a veil of injustice and violence hangs over two-thirds of humankind. A principle of auto-destruction is at work, a principle that is capable of putting a stop to the subtle physico-chemical balance and eco-logical equilibrium of the planet, and thus bringing devastation to the biosphere; and this poses a threat to the continuity of the development of the species *Homo sapiens* and *demens*.

There is a generalized attitude of neglect and disregard in the way that housing is developed. That is, it is planned for very small families who are forced to live in unhealthy conditions. Millions are condemned to live in shanty towns without proper living standards, under the permanent threat of landslides which claim thousands of victims every single year. Also, the way that important sections of the young population dress reveals decadence in taste and in culture. Many young people resort to the frequent use of violence in trying to solve personal and public affairs, which normally can be resolved through the use of dialogue and mutual understanding.

Weighed down under technological gadgets, we currently live in pitiless and senseless times. Viewed from a certain perspective it seems that we have regressed to an atrocious barbarism.

Inadequate proposals for dealing with the crisis

In the face of this situation in which there is a lack of care, many have rebelled. Their deeds and their speeches are permanently challenging the status quo. However, they are alone and they feel that they are powerless to propose a solution that can liberate them. They have lost hope.

Others have lost their faith in the human capacities for regeneration and to imagine a better future. They see the human being more in its *demens* aspect than in its *sapiens* dimension. They dwell in their own bitterness. Beyond losing one's life, is there anything worse than to lose one's will to live?

Others have faith and hope, but they propose inadequate medicines for the symptoms of a collective disease. They do not go to the real cause of the illness; they treat only the symptoms.

In this way, for instance, many propose that the widespread indisposition in civilization is the result of an abandonment of *religion*. If you forget God, they claim, everything is possible. Certainly, in modern times human beings have entered an accelerated process of secularization; they do not require God to legitimize and justify social pacts. Religion endures but it is not able to be the source of the transcendent for the whole of society.

The modern human being has produced the 'God syndrome'. The human being behaves as if he or she is God. Through the project of techno-science human beings thought they could do anything, that there would be no limits to their desire to understand everything, to dominate everything and to design everything. This desire has put enormous strains on the individual human being. The human being is not able to cope with so much development, and he or she already shows a destructive side when he or she threatens the common destiny of the Earth and its inhabitants. The 'God syndrome' has affected human beings and this condition is stressful.

It is, however, appropriate to ask here: Can religion by itself correct this deviation? Is it enough to turn people into better persons? Religion can surely revitalize an aspect of our existence, revitalize the institutional space of the sacred and emphasize its socio-historic power. But religion will not necessarily produce a way of being that is kinder and more compassionate. *Ipso facto* religion will not give rise to a form of spirituality that is capable of reconnecting[1] everything and to source everything in the original Fountain.

The crucial point does not have anything to do with religions; the crucial point has to do with the spirituality that underlies religions, which unites, connects, reconnects and integrates. Spirituality, and not religion, helps the designing of a new paradigm of civilization.

As a response to the 'God syndrome' we must propose 'the birth of God' within each person and within the history of humankind, and its epiphany in the universe.

Other groups defend the view that we must reinforce *morals* and uphold traditions in order to solve the current crisis. In the name of this proposal, millions of people mobilize themselves in defence of innocent life and against abortion, in defence of peace and against war, and in favour of a new kind of technology that is more benevolent towards the environment. Morals are important, but if they are not born out of a new definition of the human being and of its mission in the universe, if they are born without the context of a new alliance of peace and synergy* with the Earth and with the peoples that inhabit the Earth, then these morals may decline into a sort of morality that is tiresome and hypocritical and becomes an ethical nightmare. A new ethics presupposes a new perspective. It is thus important to investigate this new perspective, as I will attempt to do during the unfolding of my reflections in this book.

Others think that we require more *education*, more schooling at all levels, and more information. Obviously, it is important to share knowledge, increase the knowledge pool of humankind and democratize the processes of empowerment* of citizens. Certainly knowledge is pivotal. Without knowledge we are unable to overcome fierce enemies of humanity, such as famine, disease and miscommunication. Knowledge is empowering; knowledge empowers us. Knowledge and power have taken us to the Moon and now even beyond our solar system. But to the service of which kind of human, social and world project do we use the power of the sciences and technology? The answer to this question goes beyond the scope of science and technology. The answer to this question requires a philosophy of being and a spiritual reflection that can tell us about the meaning of all meanings and that knows how to organize human beings in such a way that they can live together under the spell of the most fundamental law of the universe. This fundamental law is synergy, the cooperation of everything with everything in a cosmic solidarity. More important than to know is never to lose the capacity always to be able to learn more. More important than the desire for power is the need for wisdom, because only wisdom will maintain power within its instrumental character and use it as a means to strengthen life and safeguard the planet.

All of these aforementioned proposals, with all their merits, do not deal with the crux of the problem. If we note, for instance, a crack on a wall it would be a mistake and irresponsible merely to patch it up with cement. Would it not be imperative to survey the foundations, which are usually invisible, and detect the causes of the crack and solve it at its source? Would not this be a more rational and wise attitude? If your child starts to show problems with her studies, if she is taking drugs, if she comes back home in the early hours of the morning, it is of no use blaming and grounding her. Perhaps the problem is not in the child; the problem may be the destroyed relationships within the family, the tension between father and mother, the financial crises faced by the parents, which frustrate the child's dreams and compromise the future of the whole family.

Inadequacies of a materialist realism

By analysing the issue in more detail, one discovers behind the edifice of scientific and technological modernity a particular philosophical view at work: *materialist realism.*

We call this philosophical view *realism* because it understands that reality exists in the form of independent objects, and as such is not dependent on the subject that observes them. However, in truth, reality is not independent. There is no object without subject and no subject without object. There is a sacred unity of reality that, like a game, always includes all as participants and never as mere spectators. So materialist realism is not very realistic because it reduces the scope of reality, as it does not include within reality the phenomena of subjectivity, conscience, life and spirituality.

From time immemorial, all peoples and cultures have had a feeling of awe when faced by the reality of the Divine that impregnates the whole of the universe; all peoples and cultures have lived the significance of the sacred in all things and cultivated spirituality as that interior visual capacity that unites all things to its divine Fountain. It is only in the last four centuries that a kind of humanity that is blind to these aspects emerged and, as such, this is a kind of humanity that is deeply impoverished in the way it realizes itself in the world. It has diminished reality to the size of our five senses, senses that are organized by analytical reasoning.

This philosophical view is also called *materialist*, 'materialist' in its ancient sense, because it presupposes that matter (atoms, elementary particles, quantum vacuum,* etc.) constitutes the one and only consistent reality; the remaining phenomena are secondary derivations of this primary reality. This philosophical view has not yet assimilated the fact that matter is not simply 'material', but is a stabilized energy that is full of complex interactions. Matter, as the philology of the word suggests, is the mother of all things, even of life, which is the self-organization* of matter. There is still no true awareness that the visible is part of the invisible.

Today the bells toll for the philosophical view called materialist realism. Quantum physics has demonstrated the strong connection of everything with everything else and the indestructible link between reality and the observer. There is no reality in itself if we disconnect the mind that relates to it; both are dimensions of the one and unique complex reality. The universe is conscious. Modern cosmology* has demonstrated that the universe is mathematically inconsistent without the existence of a Holy Spirit and of an infinitely organizing Mind.

A new philosophical view presents itself as being holistic,* ecological and spiritual. This new philosophical view offers us an alternative to materialist realism as it has the capacity to devolve to individual human beings a feeling that they are linked to the human family, to the Earth, to the universe and to the divine purpose.

In this way, this new philosophy overcomes the crucial problem that underlies the issue of carelessness: the disconnection with the Whole; the emptiness of conscience that no longer sees itself as part and parcel of the universe; the dissolution of a sacred feeling towards the cosmos and each of its entities; the unawareness of the unity of all things that is anchored in the mystery of the Supreme Creator and Provider of all things.

We must reflect on all these issues with careful attention until a time when we can develop a new form of conscience. This is the precondition if we are to develop a mature and wise attitude that can help us to search for other ways, different paths from the ones we currently tread. After centuries of a materialistic culture, we now anxiously search for a spirituality that is simple and sound, a spirituality based on the awareness of the mystery of the universe and of the human being; a spirituality based on an ethic of responsibility, solidarity and compassion; and a spirituality founded in care, in the intrinsic value of each thing, in a task well performed, in competence, in honesty and in the transparency of intentions.

Directions to the right path

It is important here to look for answers that have been inspired by other sources and other visions for the future of the planet and of humanity.

These answers are not to be found ready-made in some privileged corner of the Earth. Nor are these answers to be found in an ancient book, in sages and gurus teaching new or ancient techniques of spirituality; nor are they to be found in an ancient hidden prophecy, nor in ritualistic and magical ceremonies of initiation, nor in therapeutic procedures using natural produce. We must learn from all these answers, but we must go deeper, we must go beyond them, and we must avoid solutions sourced in a single rationale. It is important to encompass different aspects to enrich our understanding.

Following on from this last point, it could be said that answers are being formulated by all those who perform significant deeds everywhere and in every situation in the world today. Hence, there is no single departure point that is common to all these answers. There are in fact many departure points behind those answers. They are directed by a new mode of living and of acting, by a new perception of reality and by a new experience of being. They emerge from a collective path, a path that is being made as we walk.

In fact, a new paradigm* is emerging seminally, a paradigm of re-connection, of re-enchantment about nature and of compassion for those who are suffering; one sees the dawn of a renewed tenderness for life and an authentic feeling of belonging to the loving Mother Earth. This turn of events manifests itself through the growing numbers of groups that tend towards ecology, to meditation and to spirituality. We see an increase in the numbers of those who pay close attention to the impact on the environment caused by projects which are carried out by private companies or by the state; many are those who, in all these issues mentioned above, integrate the perspective that the Earth is a living and organic whole. There is an increasing number of people who seek to eat organic produce and who strictly scrutinize any level of contamination and enhancement by artificial agents or products. There is an increasing awareness that we are co-responsible for this unique planet, for its immense biodiversity and for each life threatened by extinction. There is an increasing feeling of solidarity with those populations that are decimated by famine or by natural catastrophes. One sees the mobilization of groups and public opinion in defence of the rights of animals and the social and cultural rights of human beings; one sees a remarkable effort in trying to overcome patriarchalism and in trying to strengthen the aspect of animus/anima* that is present in both men and women. One sees a remarkable effort in supporting women, and the minorities that have been socially discriminated against and which may represent millions of people, such as black populations, native populations, those who are physically handicapped, etc. Cosmic spirituality enlivens again those spirits that are sensitive to the message that emanates from the universe and nature. Religious and spiritual traditions revitalize themselves as they face the challenges of our times.

We feel the urgency for a new ethos of civilization, a new ethos that enables us to give qualitative leaps in the direction of more cooperation in our living together, a new ethos that enables us to rejuvenate our veneration for the Mystery that underlies and that supports the process of evolution.

Everywhere we see a hunger for a new alliance based on an everlasting peace with other species and with the Earth. This new social contract is forged on the respectful participation of the majority in valuing differences, in the acceptance of the various complementing issues and in an agreement built on the diversity of cultures, of means of production, of traditions and ways of life.

A new ethic from a new perspective

In critical moments such as the one in which we are currently living, it is important to revisit the ancient teachings of different peoples, and also to learn from one another. We must become apprentices and learners. It is important to devise a new ethos that allows for a new living together of human beings with other beings of the community of life, of the planet and of the cosmos; a new ethos that favours a new feeling of awe towards the majesty of the universe and towards the complexity of relations that sustain each and every being.

'Ethos' is a Greek word which, in its original sense, meant 'the burrow of an animal or a human dwelling'. In other words, ethos in its original sense referred to that part of the world that was reserved by us for us so that we could organize it, so that we could take care of it and turn it into our own habitat. We must rebuild humanity's common home, the Earth, so that all can have a place in it. It is imperative that we model our common home in a way that is sustainable and, as such, this new model will be able to support a new project of civilization. The human home is no longer the nation state; it is rather the Earth as fatherland and motherland, common to all humanity. Humanity has found itself in exile, divided by nation states, isolated by regional cultures and limited by numerous languages and dialects. Now, slowly, humanity is returning from its long exile. Humankind is meeting itself in a common place, the unified planet Earth. In this common place, humankind will make a unique history, the history of the species *Homo*, within a unique and colourful global society and sharing the understanding that we have a common destiny and the same origins.

This ethos, that is, the shaping of the human house, will embody concrete morals* – values, attitudes and practical behaviour which are synchronized with the various cultural and spiritual traditions. Despite being diverse, all moral standpoints will have the same aims; that is, to safeguard the planet, and to restore the conditions for human beings to develop and evolve ways that are increasingly more collective, interiorized and spiritualized so that the human essence is fulfilled.

From where are we to derive this new ethos for our civilization? It must emerge from the innermost part of human nature. It must emerge from dimensions that are both fundamental and comprehensible to all. If it is not born out of the very kernel of the human being, it will not possess sufficient sap to sustain the new blossoming of human beings, and as such it will not bear vigorous fruits for posterity.

We all must drink out of the same fountain. We must hear our inner nature. We must consult our true heart. Our drinking from the same fountain will overcome the halting feeling of hopelessness and bitter resignation. It should also complement those previously mentioned and incomplete pathways. In other words, drinking from the same fountain will be the basis of a new religious feeling. It will create a new ethical and moral direction. It will build a new rationality that is instrumental, emotional and spiritual, a new rationality that will transform the sciences, technology, and research into medicines for the Earth and for humanity. A new ethic will be born out of a new perspective.

What will this new perspective be? What will be this new seminal aspect of the human being, an aspect that is able to support a new historical adventure? What kind of ethos do we need? Do we need the kind of ethos that opposes carelessness, neglect and abandonment?

2

To care: the ethos of the human being

Caring is the opposite of neglect and carelessness. To care is more than a mere *act*; it is rather an *attitude*. Therefore, it encompasses more than a *moment* of awareness, of zeal and of devotion. It represents an *attitude* of activity, of concern, of responsibility and of an affective involvement with the other.

An attitude is like a fountain; it serves as the source for acts which express the attitude in the background. When we say, for instance: 'We look after our house', it is understood that a number of acts are implied; acts such as giving attention and showing concern for the people who inhabit our house. We take care of the good aura that must flood each room of the house, the bedrooms, the sitting room and the kitchen. We have zeal for the friendship that we have towards our neighbours and the warmth we show towards our guests. We show devotion towards our house, so that it becomes a well-loved place, a place that we long for when we are away and that fills us with joy when we return. We maintain a basic and vigilant approach towards the physical state of the house, its grounds and its garden. We look after the cat, the dog, the fish, and the birds that settle in our trees. All of these are part of the material, personal, social, ecological and spiritual attitudes of caring for the house.

'To care' as a fundamental mode-of-being

However, 'to care' is something more than merely an act or an attitude among other attitudes. Martin Heidegger

14

(1889–1976), the philosopher who better realized the fundamental importance of taking care, wrote in his famous book *Being and Time*: 'Care, as a primordial structural totality, lies "before" ["Vor"] every factical "attitude" and "situation" of Dasein, and it does so existentially *a priori*; this means that it always lies *in* them.'[1] That is, 'to care' is at the very root of the human being; it is there before anyone does anything. And if someone does do anything it is always accompanied by, and permeated with, a caring attitude. This means that we must acknowledge that the attitude of taking care is a fundamental mode-of-being, which is always present and which cannot be removed from reality. It is a fountainhead, an original and ontological* aspect which it is impossible to totally disregard.

A mode-of-being is not a new being. It is a way of self-structuring and self-knowledge that the being itself has. 'To care' is part of the nature and of the constitution of the human being. The mode-of-being 'to care' reveals in a concrete manner the way the human being really is.

Without this aspect the human being ceases to be a human being. If the human being is not cared for from cradle to grave, the human being becomes unstructured, wastes away, loses its bearings in life and dies. If, during life, the human being does not do with care everything it engages with, it will end up jeopardizing itself and destroying that which is around it. It is for this very reason that 'to care' must be understood as part of the human essence, and this fact answers the very question: What is it to be a human being? 'To care' ought to be present in everything. In the words of Martin Heidegger: 'With the expression "care" we have in mind a basic existential-ontological phenomenon'.[2] In other words, 'to care' is a phenomenon that stands as the enabling source of human existence qua human.

We can answer in various and different ways the question: What is the human being? This question and its possible answers are dependent on a social understanding, on the different ways of seeing the world, on the diversity of philosophical views, scientific paradigms and projects that have been elaborated by the ingenious character of the human being. A latent and unconscious answer, however, becomes overt and conscious when we pose the following question: What kind of image of the human being is inscribed in a culture, like ours, that privileges scientific and technical rationality above all? The natural answer will be: the human being is a rational animal. What kind of image is hidden in the capitalist mode of production and in an economy that is solely based on market forces? The obvious answer is: the human being is necessarily a being of necessities, a hungry animal, with needs that must be met, and as such the human being is a consuming being. What kind of image of the human being underlies the ideal of democracy? The answer to this question will be: the human being is a participative being, a social actor, a subject with a personal and collective history who seeks to build social relations that are egalitarian, fair, free and fraternal, which maximizes their potential within the determinate historical and social conditions of the time. What idea of the human being is presupposed in the fight for human rights? The answer will surely be: the human being is gifted with sacredness because it is subject to rights and duties that are inalienable and because it presents itself as an infinite project. What kind of understanding of the human being is present in the technical and scientific project of the domination of nature? The most probable answer will be: the human being understands itself as the apex of the evolutionary process (which is an illusion), the centre of all forms of being (anthropocentrism), and considers that everything else, and especially nature, only has value with reference to the human being, and as such the human being can treat everything else as it judges fit. When the mystic St John of the Cross says that the human being is called to be a participant with God, what kind of image does this pre-suppose of the human being? The audacious answer will be: the human being has the capacity to dialogue with the Mystery of the world, to ask for an ultimate Sense and to enter into communion with, and be one with, God. Lastly, what kind of image of the human being do we project when we discover the human being as a being-in-the-world-with-others always in relation, building his habitat, occupied with things, concerned with people, willing to suffer with and be happy with those to whom he feels united and whom he loves? The most adequate answer to this question will be: the human being is a being that takes care; moreover, his essence is found in caring. To have an attitude of care towards all that he plans and does is the essential characteristic of the human being.

It is always important to explain the image of the human being that underlies our understanding of the world, our projects and our practices. Only in this way can we be conscious of what we want to be and only in this manner can we continuously submit this image to criticism and to a possible improvement.

Humanity has opened many pathways in its pursuit to decipher the essence of the human being. Humanity has made use of the arts, of paintings in rocky caves, of drawings on clay vases. Humanity expressed itself in great monuments, in ivory miniatures and in a vast array of folk songs. It utilized the word through myths, fables, poems and narratives. It used cognition through philosophy and cosmological views. Religions offered the most audacious interpretations of human nature through the myths of creation, of the end of the world and of the origins of human beings. Nowadays, the use of cinema, of the virtual universe of communication, and especially of the empirical, hermeneutical and holistic sciences is preferred. All these have an implicit anthropology; that is, a particular understanding of human beings, men and women.

Myths: an ancient knowledge of the human essence

All the issues mentioned above are of great importance. Whenever possible I shall try to incorporate them into the various parts of this book. However, I shall favour one particular path, the path of myths. I shall favour this path because I understand that mythologies, along with religions, provide a far better explanation about human nature than do the sciences and philosophies. It is in myths that, generation after generation, cultures have projected great visions; it is in myths that cultures have accumulated reflections; and it is in myths that cultures have developed their understanding. It is through myths that cultures have handed down these visions, reflections and understandings to their future generations. Cultures learned to use language in an artistic manner, to use language with images that come straight from the depths of a collective unconscious that is accessible to all ages and at all times. Beyond its images and symbols, myths arose and continue to give rise to many emotions. And it is these emotions that remain and mobilize individuals and peoples throughout history.

It is not certain that we in modern times with our instrumental rationality, with all our tradition of empirical research, criticism and accumulation of knowledge about practically everything, know more about the human being than the ancient creators of myths. These myth creators have revealed themselves to be meticulous observers and extremely wise in every situation and on every existential issue. It is necessary for us to revisit them, to appreciate their contributions and to listen to their messages, which are always relevant.

I will thus pursue the path leading to myths. And as such, it is important here to correctly understand what myths are. Myths are not things of an ancient past, random outcomes of primitive thinking, or uncontrollable fantasies. A myth is always relevant and, as such, we in modern times also create myths.

A myth is a sort of language that translates deep inner phenomena which are indescribable by analytical rationality. How are we to speak about falling in love, about love, about an essential form of caring, about the treason of a loved one, about crises in life, about deadly diseases, about birth and death, without emotions and without telling exemplary stories? Abstract and cold concepts cannot translate the colours of reality; they cannot produce spectacles in the imagination. And as such, and in a peculiar manner, they falsify our experience of phenomena.

As it has been said, the current consecrated language of scientific psychology represents to a certain extent an insult to the soul because in the elaboration of its instruments of analysis it leaves out powerful energies; it leaves out real gods and goddesses that inhabit the inner depths of the human being, and it also leaves out images and symbols. Scientific psychology prefers abstract concepts, which have been extracted from a paradigm that favours physics and mechanics. We must thus learn to combine the analytical and instrumental rationality that provides us with a scientific rigour with the emotional and cordial rationality that gives us the imaginary and the myths.

The mythological goddesses and gods should not be considered as existing in themselves, as substantial beings that are independent of our reality. They represent archetypes* of the collective unconscious mind; that is, they are centres of great energy and meaning that can be expressed properly only through the language of heroes and heroines and of gods and goddesses. They are figures loaded with emotion, turned into paradigmatic reference points that represent inspirations for human behaviour.

Polytheism does not represent an inferior stage of the religious evolution towards monotheism. If it is properly understood it does not necessarily seek to affirm the multiplicity of deities; it rather seeks to affirm the numerous faces of the one and only Deity, of the one and only Mystery of communion that is linked to the exposed dynamism of the world and of the spirit. Monotheism, on the other hand, walks at a steady pace towards a grand and united vision that impoverishes the many aspects of the sacred.

If one understands the multiple deities as powerful spiritual forces, then one sees that they represent the various energetic centres and the different fountains of senses that structure human subjectivity. The Divine inhabits this subjectivity, and for this very reason we are spiritual beings; we are spiritual beings on top of being corporeal and mental entities. Spiritually and mentally we are not monotheists; rather we are pluralists. We possess many vital centres and not only one. Nor are we dominated by only one of these centres; be it rationality, power, desire or the heart, none of these centres dominates. We are permeated and wrapped in many of these energies; they make human life dynamic and also dramatic. All of them are thus articulated in the particular existence of each person. It is through all of these energies that we have access to the supreme Energy that inhabits the universe and the human heart.

In this book I want to analyse a particular fable-myth that tells us about the human essence in a way that is relevant to the critical problems of our times. This is the fable-myth about care. It is in the attitude of taking care that we will find the necessary ethos for human sociability. It is in this attitude that we will recognize the source of the very essence of human beings, men and women. When I speak of ethos I mean the collection of values, principles and inspirations that give origin to acts and attitudes (and morals) that will give rise to the common ground that will be shared by us all, and to the new society that is emerging. There is urgency in the need for a new ethos of care, of synergy, of re-connection, of benevolence, of long-lasting peace with the Earth, with life, with society, with the fate of people, and especially with the great majority of the peoples of the Earth, who are impoverished and condemned.

3

The fable-myth about 'care'

The fable-myth about essential care was originally written
in Latin and bears Greek influences. It gained its final literary
expression just prior to the beginning of the Christian era in
Rome. Let us now look at the original Latin text of this fable-
myth about care, and then at its English translation.

> Cura cum fluvium transiret, vidit cretosum lutum
> sustulitque cogitabunda atque coepit fingere.
> dum deliberat quid iam fecisset, Jovis intervenit.
> rogat eum Cura ut det illi spiritum, et facile impetrat.
> cui cum vellet Cura nomen ex sese ipsa imponere,
> . Jovis prohibuit suumque nomen ei dandum esse dictitat.
> dum Cura et Jovis disceptant, Tellus surrexit simul
> suumque nomen esse volt cui corpus praebuerit suum.
> sumpserunt Saturnum iudicem, is sic aecus iudicat:
> 'tu Jovis quia spiritum dedisti, in morte spiritum,
> tuque Tellus, quia dedisti corpus, corpus recipito,
> Cura eum quia prima finxit, teneat quamdiu vixerit.
> sed quae nunc de nomine eius vobis controversia est,
> homo vocetur, quia videtur esse factus ex humus.'[1]

This is the English translation of the original:

> Once when 'Care' was crossing a river, she saw some clay; she
> thoughtfully took up a piece and began to shape it. While
> she was meditating on what she had made, Jupiter came by. 'Care'
> asked him to give it spirit, and this he gladly granted. But when
> she wanted her name to be bestowed upon it, he forbade this,
> and demanded that it be given his name instead. While 'Care'
> and Jupiter were disputing, Earth arose and desired that her name

21

be conferred on the creature, since she had furnished it with part of her body. They asked Saturn to be their arbiter, and he made the following decision, which seemed a just one: 'Since you, Jupiter, have given it spirit, you shall receive that spirit at its death; and since you, Earth, have given its body, you shall receive its body. But since 'Care' first shaped this creature, she shall possess it as long as it lives. And because there is now a dispute among you as to its name, let it be called '*homo*', for it is made out of *humus* [earth].[2]

This fable-myth is the departing point for my reflections on 'caring'. I shall demonstrate that 'to care' is in the very essence of the human being. But prior to doing this, let us acquaint ourselves with the author of this inspiring literary work.

4

An ingenious slave:
Gaius Julius Hyginus

Myths do not have an author; they belong to the common wisdom of humanity, which is preserved by the collective unconscious in the form of great symbols, archetypes and of exemplary figures. In each generation this wisdom emerges to the conscience in the form of a thousand facets, and through these many facets it always transmits the same essential message. It enlightens pathways and it inspires practices. There are moments in history, however, in which the myth gains a classical formulation. Hesiod in Greece (at the beginning of the seventh century BCE), Ovid in Rome (43 BCE–17 CE), the brothers Grimm in Germany (1785–1863 CE), and Luís Câmara Cascudo in Brazil (1898–1986 CE) were a few of these inspired scribes.

It was just like this that the fable-myth of essential care happened, a fable-myth which is also known as the 'Fable of Hyginus'.* As I have maintained, what is important is not the author of the narrative of the myth but the meaning contained in the narrative. Despite this fact, it is still interesting to know who Hyginus was and why Hyginus himself has become a mythical figure.

The saga of Hyginus

His full name is Gaius Julius Hyginus.[1] Let us now explore the context of his appearance.

The year 44 BCE was on course and Gaius Julius Caesar (100–44 BCE), famous general, consul and founder of the dynasty of Roman Caesars, had been assassinated in the middle of the

Senate by his adoptive son Brutus. To succeed him a triumvirate was created, consisting of three consuls: his adoptive grandchild Gaius Julius Caesar Octavianus ('Octavian' and later 'Caesar Augustus'; 63 BCE–14 CE), Marcus Antonius ('Mark Antony'; 83–30 BCE) and Marcus Emilius Lepidus (who died in the year 12 BCE).

Soon enough the three of them had a disagreement and each of them sought absolute power. Octavian, more shrewd and astute, overcame his two opponents. In the year 27 BCE he proclaimed himself emperor and also appropriated to himself the title *Augustus*, which up to that date had been reserved only for the gods. From that date onwards he was called Caesar Augustus. It was during his reign that Jesus Christ was born, a fact that does not lack importance for Christians.

In the year 47 BCE, still in the middle of the dispute over power, Octavian entered victoriously into Alexandria, the great city in the north of Egypt that was famous for its culture, its philosophical schools and its library. It was during this time that Octavian met Hyginus, a youngster who was considered a brilliant intellect and possessed a vast knowledge despite being only 22 years old. Octavian was so impressed that he decided to take Hyginus back with him to Rome.

As often happened in those days all victorious generals could take as slaves any persons that aroused their interest. These slaves were very often instructors of languages and Greek culture to their children. As a public sign of ownership the owner's own name was imposed on these slaves. It was like this with Hyginus. His name was changed to Gaius Julius Hyginus, though historically he is simply known as Hyginus.

In Rome, after some time, Augustus freed him but kept him in his service. Augustus sent him to the best school of the day, a school headed by Alexander Polihistor, who was an old slave of Alexandria and who had also been freed by Augustus. Alexander Polihistor was director of the famous Palatine Library which had been founded by Augustus in the year 28 BCE.

The libraries in those ancient times were more than our current libraries. They are equivalent to the cultural foundations or academies of today. In the ancient libraries one did not merely find books, one also found courses of all kinds, courses that ranged through theology, history, botany and even astrology. In the libraries, philosophical disputes and intellectual meetings of poets and historians very often occurred.

In an ambience that favoured cultural flourishing, Hyginus made a brilliant career. Excited by his old slave Alexander, Caesar Augustus, who kept an eye on everything, put Hyginus in charge of the Appolinis Library. This appointment meant that Hyginus could set his own courses and organize intellectual activities since he now had direct access to the most prominent spirits of the day and to the many books of the library. He was then only 30 years old.

With the death of Alexander Polihistor, Caesar Augustus appointed Hyginus director of the central library; that is, of the Palatine Library. From that day onwards, for more than 40 years, Hyginus enlivened the cultural life of Rome. It is said that he kept working even at the age of 70.

The great poet Ovid (43 BCE–17 CE) was a close friend of his. Virgil himself (70–19 BCE), who is considered the greatest Latin poet, was his pupil.

According to historians, Hyginus died in poverty in the year 10 CE, through a failure to administer his own affairs. Ovid, in solidarity with his misfortunes, dedicated an ode to him entitled '*Tristia Hyginus*', which could be translated as 'The disappointments of Hyginus'.

The works of Hyginus

Hyginus made good use of his contacts and the sources in the library to write numerous works. He produced theological texts covering the characteristics of the gods (*De proprietatibus deorum*), and more specifically about household gods (*De dis penatibus*). He specialized in biographies, publishing six tomes about the lives and works of illustrious people of the world and of Rome (*De vita rebusque illustrium virorum* and *De viribus illustribus urbis Romae*). He also dedicated himself to the study of ecology and made detailed geographical descriptions of Italian cities (*De situ urbium Italicorum*) and agriculture. He wrote the first known paper on bees (*De apibus*) and also wrote on astronomy and astrology (*De mundi et sphaerae; De signorum coelestium historiis; De astrologia*). As one may gather, Hyginus was a man of little rest and numerous intellectual interests.

His main work that is of direct interest for us here is entitled *Fables or Genealogies (Fabulae seu Genealogiae)*. This work is a compilation of about 300 legends, histories and myths of the Greek and Latin traditions. It is a vast work, which is however inconsistent. It contains material of the most diverse origins and in different styles; it even contains contradictions. For this reason it was argued that the book of fables was not solely written by Hyginus. It was thought that as Hyginus was a knowledgeable and refined person he could not have committed the errors and contradictions that are present in the work. These errors and contradictions must be present thanks to the interfering of other hands in the original text.

Another school of thought, however, has a different interpretation: Hyginus had respected the materials as he had found them, merely compiling and formatting them. Certainly, some of the materials had indeed been reworked by Hyginus with great care and aesthetic attention, since he was a refined master of this.

This is what seems to have happened to fable-myth number 220, which I have mentioned previously. Its origins are said to be Greek; it was however rewritten by Hyginus in terms that suited the Roman culture. It became very concise and of great literary beauty.

In the next chapter I seek to analyse the anthropological, philosophical and aesthetic aspects of the account of the fable-myth of Care.

5

Explaining the fable-myth about care

Let me now explain the characters of this beautiful fable-myth. Such an inquiry will provide us with some basic elements which will enlighten the nature of the human essence and set the foundations for an ethos for a new era.

What is a fable? What is a myth?

Before proceeding any further let me explain my understanding of what a fable and a myth are.

Fable is an imaginary narrative in which the characters are, as a rule, animals, plants, or personifications of qualities, virtues and vices, and in which the main objective is to transmit moral lessons or to make an abstract truth concrete. Well known are the fables of La Fontaine (1621–95), such as, for instance, the fable about the fox and the grapes.

In the case that concerns us here, Hyginus takes the dimension 'care' and personifies it. 'Care' takes a walk along the beach, sees a piece of clay, starts to imagine what can be done with it and ends up moulding the piece of clay into a dummy. 'Care' has an argument with Jupiter and with Tellus, and honours the judgement of Saturn.

This fable is woven through with Greco-Latin mythological figures of great symbolic meaning, such as Jupiter, Tellus and Saturn. For this very reason this fable is called a fable-myth. What is a myth?

Myth is something very complex because of the ambiguities that it contains. In the common language of mass communication, a myth can convey a reductionist, concealed and self-centred vision of reality. As such it is equivalent to an ideology. Thus, myth designates sayings or collective creeds about relevant themes (people, situations, happenings) that circulate in the culture. In this way we hear about 'the myth of the good savage', 'the myth of the weaker sex' and 'the myth of the lazy black man'.

The expression 'the myth of the good savage' seeks to transmit the belief that the indigenous Indian of the Americas is a savage who is always good because he is a being in the state of nature uncontaminated by culture. This expression represents a reductionist view because the indigenous Indians of the Americas have their own culture, they intervene in their own way with nature, and as social beings they have symbolic and diabolical dimensions.

Patriarchal society has qualified women as weak and as such it has forged the myth of the weaker sex, which is untrue. A woman has her own way of being strong, and in this case muscular strength does not count. In the way she deals with children from their conception, during the crises that happen along the way, her presence throughout the children's lives, and especially her running of the complexities of a household and her capacity for tolerating suffering and overcoming obstacles, in all these, a woman shows that her strength and tenacity leave men far behind. In many aspects woman is the stronger sex and man the weaker one.

The charge that the black man is lazy, beyond being a falsehood, is also slander. Almost everything that has been built in lands where slavery was practised, such as Brazil, Colombia, the Caribbean, and the south of the United States, has been built through the workmanship of the black slave. Black men and women showed great diligence despite the fact that they were treated as 'goods', charcoal to be used up in the machinery of production. Moreover, this group, possibly more than any other, has infused values in Brazilian and

North-American culture with elements that range from cuisine, music and language to kindness in relations with people, and also mysticism. They, despite being slaves, were civilizing agents.

Myth, for another school of thought, is the same as mere fantasy or a distorted interpretation of reality. As such, myth is that which is opposed to reality. In this way, for instance, the highly proclaimed good effects of artificial sweeteners on the body are, for serious nutritionists, a myth and not a reality: on the one hand artificial sweeteners do not possess calories, on the other they speed up the process that weakens the neurons and as such they open the way for a quicker loss of mental capacities. The expression 'myth-maniac' is used of one who has an obsession with creating 'myths', fictitious happenings, factoids,[1] or one who has an obsession with projecting inconceivable interpretations upon reality.

I do not subscribe to any of these characterizations since they do not help to understand the phenomenon I wish to analyse. In fact, modern disciplines criticize these characterizations of myth; modern disciplines, especially philosophy, anthropology, deep psychology and modern theology, rather confer myth with a very positive depiction.

For instance, the Jungian psychoanalytic school affirms that someone has become a myth when they have lived a biography (i.e. an existential narrative or saga) with such density that many people rediscover themselves within it or through it see ideals or ancient dreams being fulfilled. As such, we speak of Pelé as a football myth, of Charles Chaplin as a cinematographic myth, of Princess Diana as a media myth, of Mahatma Gandhi as an ethical-political myth, and of Dom Hélder Câmara[2] or Martin Luther King as a prophetic-religious myth. All these people have become transformed themselves into powerful symbols; that is to say, they have become myths capable of crystallizing collective energies, of making a direct connection with people and mobilizing the masses.

Moreover, the anthropology and philosophy of symbolic forms have demonstrated that myth is tantamount to an autonomous form of thinking, which is set apart from reasoning. It is as legitimate as any other form of thinking. It is an expression of emotional intelligence, which is distinct from functional intelligence. This latter, functional intelligence, informs about objects; it is utilitarian, it makes calculations, it is instrumental; it is the weapon of the science and of the technique, it is indispensable for the functioning of life on a day-to-day basis. The former, emotional intelligence, uses images, symbols, parables, stories and myths to evoke inner feelings, to express that which gives meaning and value to the human being; it touches the heart and provokes emotions. Poets, religious and spiritual masters such as Jesus, Isaiah, Muhammad, Buddha, the Sufi mystic Rumi, Pope John XXIII, the Dalai Lama, and others have made use of emotional intelligence. And in the same way modern means of communication, particularly through strategies of marketing and of advertising, also make use of emotional intelligence.

Usually myth is communicated through the use of narratives that utilize powerful symbols and representations, such as gods and goddesses, confrontations between the heavens and the Earth, to express true happenings or histories loaded with drama and meaning, true happenings or histories which have always been experienced by humanity. Or they seek to explain the advent of realities that, for certain communities, have special significance and value, such as the name of a place, the importance of a certain animal or mountain, or of a certain exemplary way of good or evil behaviour. Myth always represents depictions of the collective consciousness, which are told and retold throughout the generations.

Joseph Campbell, a modern expert on myths, wisely said: 'Dreams are private myths; the myths are shared dreams.' Not without reason, the founder of depth psychology Carl Gustav Jung (1875–1961) understood myth as a way of becoming aware of archetypes of the collective unconscious. That is: myths represent the appearance of images of great experiences, of dreams, of fears (archetypes) that humanity has elaborated historically during its long process of individualization. Myths emerge in the consciousness of people and of communities. They reveal metamorphoses that unfold hidden forces, and as such they give these forces historical actuality. They help to understand the universality of certain experiences and they point the way to the various crossing points that characterize the human adventure.

Some exemplary myths and fables

To illustrate these theoretical reflections it is appropriate here to provide two factual examples of myths in the sense that I have just explained above. One example comes from the Greeks, the other from one of the peoples of the Brazilian jungle.

The Greek myth of Eros, the god of love, is well known. Love is renowned for being the original force of the universe. According to this myth, love is prior to the heavens and the Earth. In its most ancient version, Eros was born out of chaos* and night. Therefore, Eros was born out of a prior reality, a reality that is more essential. Night hatched a fecund egg, and from this egg Eros, love, was born. From the two halves of the egg's shell the heavens (Uranus) and the Earth (Gaia*) appeared. Because of Eros, the heavens and the Earth fell in love, united themselves, and generated all things that exist in the world. These things, in turn, also felt attracted to each other, and fell in love. They sought to unite themselves in love. Eros, therefore, is responsible for diversity (i.e. heavens, Earth, and all things) and at the same time he is also responsible for the unity of all things (i.e. the attraction that every thing, people and objects, feel for each other).

Another very beautiful myth is the Tupi[3] myth of *mandioca*,[4] a basic food source of many indigenous cultures. It is said that one day a long time ago an Indian chief had a granddaughter. Her skin was as white as the whitest cloud. Mandi was her name. Everyone was intrigued and found it intimidating when they saw the colour of Mandi's skin. In the tribe, people started looking at each other, comparing the golden-brown colour of their skins with the fairness of the beautiful girl. They believed that this happening was a bad omen. Then, with some force, they asked the Indian chief to do away with his granddaughter. However, full of love and compassion, he delayed such cruelty day after day, until in the dead of the early hours of one morning, he went to the river, taking his granddaughter with him. He washed her carefully. The following day he gathered the whole tribe and said with a strong voice so as to avoid objections that the spirits had recommended that Mandi should remain with them and that she should be well treated by the whole tribe. The Indians, still doubtful, obeyed and left things as they were. With the passing of time, Mandi grew up with such graciousness that everyone forgot the bad omen and ended up being captivated by her. The Indian chief was very proud and happy. Suddenly, one day, however, Mandi died. Her parents, knowing how much her grandfather, the chief, loved her, buried her in their communal hut. But he was inconsolable, and he shut himself in his pain and cried all the time. He cried day and night over the tomb of his dear Mandi. So many were his tears that from the ground a small plant sprouted. The birds came around to pick on it and became intoxicated. It is said in the myth that one day the ground opened up to show the beautiful roots of the plant, which were produced by the weeping of the grandfather. The Indians respectfully collected the roots and soon realized that they were as white as Mandi's skin, and when they ate these roots they found that they were delicious. It was in this way that these roots became the main food supply of the Tupi Indians. They called these roots *mandioca*, which means 'the body of Mandi'.

As we can understand from these two examples, the myth expresses values of great importance, but which cannot be expressed properly through the use of concepts. In this way, stories are created. Stories are narratives loaded with emotion, symbols and representations to provide explanations of mysteries and important facts. And as in the above-mentioned cases they provided an explanation for the mystery of love and of the importance of *mandioca* in the diet of the peoples that inhabit the Amazon jungle. This is the richness of the myth. One rediscovers oneself in the great myths, or finds explanations for essential realities such as love and food.

Something very similar happens with care. Care is so important for human life and the preservation of all kinds of life that it has given origin to a fable-myth. Care is personified and becomes a concrete being. As such, Care moulds the clay, holds a conversation with the heavens (Jupiter) and with the Earth (Tellus). It calls up the supreme authority of the god of heavens and Earth, the god who founded the golden age and the absolute Utopia of human beings (Saturn). The fable-myth of Care as elaborated by Hyginus wants to express the meaning of care for human life. At the moment of the appearance of human life, those most important universal forces were at work: the heavens (Jupiter), the Earth (Tellus), and history and Utopia (Saturn).

The fable-myth of Care, moreover, represents an experience that has been observed in many cultures of the West and the East: the creation of a human being from the clay of the Earth, moulded from *humus*, which means the fertile soil. From the word *humus* we get our word 'human', the son or daughter of the fecund Earth, as is well described in the narrative. Something similar is present in the first two chapters of Genesis: Adam is made out of the clay of the Earth. The Hebrew word for 'earth' is *Adamah*. From the word *Adamah* we get the word 'Adam', which means the son and daughter of the Earth.

The fable-myth also observes that human beings cannot be solely interpreted from the perspective of the Earth (Tellus). The human being possesses something of the heavens, the divine (Jupiter) and, for this reason, the narrative tells that the piece of clay does not remain inert. It has received from the divinity the principle of life, the spirit. Only as such is it really a complete human being. It is Jupiter, the supreme divinity, who infuses this spirituality into the human being. It is appropriate here to ask the questions: Who is Jupiter? Who is Tellus?

The heavenly dimension: Jupiter

Jupiter is the principal divinity of Roman religion. He is the god who created the heavens and the Earth, the gods and human beings. Perhaps the philology of the word 'Jupiter' may disclose the kind of experience that is behind it. Behind the word 'Jupiter' is hidden the particle *jou*, which is derived from the Sanskrit word *dew* that means light, brightness and clarity. *Piter*, which is also present in 'Jupiter', is the ancient formulation of the word *pater*, father. Jupiter, therefore, means the father and lord of light. And from the Sanskrit root *dyew*, which is present in the Greek language, in the Lithuanian language, and in the Latin, Germanic and Celtic languages, we get the words *Deus* (God) and *dia* (day). Within this context, the word *Deus* refers to an experience of light. Light with its brightness and warmth constitutes one of the fundamental experiences of the psyche. It embodies the meaning and joy of life, the recognition in the crowd of the face of a loved one, the appreciation of the splendour of nature and of the stars, the identification of a path and of freeing oneself from the anguish of the darkness and of wandering. To wish someone *bom dia* (good day), originally meant to wish someone a *bom deus* (good god) and a lot of light in his or her paths. Who nowadays still recalls the sacred memory, which is present in an expression that is so trivial as *bom dia* (good day)?

Jupiter manifests himself in the religious life of the Romans through the glory of the day, and also through the rays of light, and lightning and thunder in the storms (*Jupiter Tonans*, Jupiter the Thunderer). It was within this context that Jupiter was combined with Zeus, the major god of the Greek pantheon, since he possessed the same meaning. The name 'Zeus' also derives from the Sanskrit *dyew pitar* or from *dyaus pitar*, which means father of the luminous heaven and of the sunny day.

Agriculture is extremely dependent on light and on atmospheric phenomena such as cold and heat, rain and wind. For this reason Jupiter was venerated as the protector and promoter of agriculture. From agriculture, in the past and in the present day, comes the food for life. Jupiter has to do with the production and reproduction of the mystery of life, and as such he was revered as the main divinity.

As Jupiter represented the supreme god so the Roman emperors used to put themselves under his protection, or even claimed to represent his power, his justice and his right and law. Some, such as Augustus (63 BCE–14 CE) and ironically Nero (37–68 CE), felt themselves to be the incarnation of the god Jupiter.

When Jupiter appears in the fable-myth of Care he comes represented as the creator and giver of life and spirit. He represents the plenitude of the divine; that is to say, he represents the dimension that transcends reality.

The earthly dimension: Tellus

The goddess Tellus has gained a special importance in the fable-myth of Hyginus. In all cultures, as in the case of the Greco-Roman tradition, the Earth is one of the central myths. She has received many names: Gaia/Tellus, Demeter/Ceres, Hestia/Vesta. And I shall come back to this point below.

Before proceeding, however, it is important to note that in very ancient social pieces of evidence from the Palaeolithic period, and thus more than 40,000 years ago, when matriarchal* societies were in force, the universe was represented as a great mother figure, as *Mater Mundi*. She, herself, and without the aid of anyone else, generated everything: the heavens, the gods, human beings and all of the remaining beings in nature. In the head of this figure, this living organism, figured the starry heavens; in her breast, the Earth where human life is found; and below, in the *anus mundi*, the anus of the world, the place where the underworld figured.

In a subsequent stage under the aegis of patriarchal societies – that is, from the Neolithic period onwards and thus about 10,000 years ago – a simpler representation of the goddess was elaborated. The Earth is not sensed anymore as an absolute reality. She is, together with the heavens, a part of reality. She represents the Great Mother, the *Magna Mater*, the *Bona Mater*, here below; she is the wife of the Great Father from up there in the heavens. As all human mothers, she gives birth, nurtures, defends and continuously gives life. She always unites and opposes herself to the other part of the whole, the Father of the heavens, the *Pater Coelorum*. From the marriage between heaven and Earth, however, all things originated. The heavens represent the masculine principle, the semen, the seed, and the organizing element. The Earth represents the feminine principle, the uterus that receives the semen, the sheltering and accepting principle. Both, in their own way, are active principles.

Three mythological figures of the Greco-Roman mythology that are woven through our Western culture represent the mystery of the Earth. In the Greek version these are Gaia, Demeter and Hestia. And their Roman correspondents are Tellus, Ceres and Vesta. These figures have to do with experiences that we also have today.

Gaia/Tellus (who is also referred to as 'Geia' since the origin of the word is *ge* which means earth, and *aia* which means great, and thus the two versions Gaia and Geia), the

Great Mother, represents the planet Earth as a living whole and producer of life.

Demeter/Ceres represents that part of the planet Earth that has been cultivated. And it is here that human collaboration enters with its workmanship and art of cultivation. She was the goddess of sowing. From Ceres we get our word 'cereal'.

Lastly, Hestia/Vesta symbolizes that part of the planet Earth which we reserve and demarcate for the constitution of the human home. At the heart of all Roman homes there was a fire that burnt night and day. This fire was the sign of Hestia; it was the sign that there was life, comfort and shelter in the house.

Gaia/Tellus, Demeter/Ceres and Hestia/Vesta were the affectionate references through which the Greeks and Romans elaborated their ecology; that is to say, their reverential relationship with the environment. Everything was loaded with respect and veneration because they did not see things as simple and inert beings; they rather saw things full of connections and meaning. The Earth, in its various expressions of Great Mother, cultivated earth and home, was sensed as a living organism. This organism cannot be violated and wrecked. If it is then it avenges itself through storms, lightning, droughts, fires, earthquakes and volcanoes.

The human being maintained a relationship of veneration and fear towards Mother Earth. This feeling has never been totally lost in humanity. There have always been people who have been drawn to the magic and the incantations of nature, even during the age of the rise of modern science, which deconsecrated and reduced the world to a source of resources to be explored by technology. Nowadays that ancient feeling about the world has reappeared in the so-called sciences of the Earth. They also tend increasingly to see the Earth as Gaia, a superorganism alive, highly organized and with a finely tuned balance, always fragile and constantly rebuilding itself. Such is the theory of Gaia, which was put forward by the scientist from NASA, James Lovelock, a theory that proposes a new (and truly ancient) way of seeing the Earth, of seeing the Earth as a living organism. Departing from scientific and empirical data, James Lovelock and others want to express the same thing that those ancient myths expressed through intuition and communion; that is, the Earth is alive and produces all forms of life.

In the fable-myth of Hyginus, the Earth appears to claim to be the most ancient. She furnished Care with the material from which Care moulded the human being, the clay. The goddess Tellus/Earth represents the dimension Earth, the immanent aspect of reality.

The historical dimension and Utopia: Saturn

And lastly, to put an end to the conflict between the heavens (Jupiter) and the Earth (Tellus), Saturn is called. Who is he? Why call specifically Saturn and not another god? Is not Jupiter the supreme god? It could be presumed that Saturn is above Jupiter himself since he must mediate the dispute in which Jupiter is involved. And in fact it is just like this, as I shall demonstrate below.

The myth of Saturn is one of the most complex myths of ancient mythology. Within this myth many mythological schools, such as the Italic, Etruscan, Greek, Orphic-Pithagoric and Roman, merge and overlap. This complexity reveals a profound significance for understanding human life. I shall deal below only with the aspects of the myth of Saturn that are relevant to the fable-myth of Hyginus.

One of the first indications of its original meaning comes from the name Saturn itself. Saturn comes from *satus*, which means 'sowed' and which comes from the verb *serere*, to sow, to plant. Saturn is the god of sowing and of agriculture, a god which is typically Italian and Mediterranean. His importance is further revealed in the greatest of the Roman festivals, the Saturnalia. This festival was a true carnival. Everything stopped: work, schools, courts and the carrying out of punishments and fines. Whatever was normally forbidden on other days was permitted during the week of Saturnalia. There was an inversion of roles: the slaves dressed themselves as masters, and the masters served them. Eating, drinking, dancing and singing turned into carnival-like parades under the sceptre of the King of Saturnalia, *Princeps Saturnalici*, a true *Rei Momo*,[5] who was chosen annually.

There was an expectation about the great political Utopia of humanity: the encounter with the myth of the golden age and of the lost paradise which would be met through the path of festivities and of the collective unconscious. According to this myth originally there were no social classes, no laws, no crimes, and no prisons; everyone lived in plenitude of freedom, justice, peace, superabundance and happiness, and as brothers and sisters at home. This awesome memory was never lost in the conscience of humanity, and it remains to this day – be it something from the past to be recovered, be it something to be realized in the future. This Utopia mobilizes groups, creates ideologies, and feeds the imagination of human beings who do not tire of dreaming of a future of reconciliation and integration of human society. Societies and their citizens cannot live without this dream of Utopia; otherwise these societies and their citizens become victims of mean bearers of power, who make use of this power for their own benefit without any perspective of well-being for all of society. The god Saturn incorporated all those values, which were celebrated in a festival of remembrance of the golden age. The modern carnivals, especially the one in Brazil, still keep this ancient memory.

Because of these festivals, the Roman god Saturn was combined with the Greek god Kronos. Kronos was the most ancient god of the earliest utopia of a happy society. There were also festivals dedicated to Kronos that bore the same theme of recovering the golden age, freedom, equality as brothers and sisters, and the inversion of roles. These were the Kronia and they were equivalent to the Saturnalias. Kronos/Saturn was the ancient god, a god prior to Jupiter. He was the first king of gods, lord of the heavens and of the earth. He reigned in the Fortune Islands. There lived the fortunate ones in a kingdom of peace, justice, joviality and abundance. This was the golden age, an age in which the rivers were of milk and nectar and in which the earth produced everything without the need of the labour and sweat of the peasants. This golden age was sung of by the Roman poet Ovid as 'the eternal springtime in which the winds with their sweet breath caressed the flowers begotten without the need of seeds'.

The myth of the golden age, presided over by Kronos/ Saturn, represents the major Utopia, the ideal of a humanity socially integrated. As such it was given attention by the philosopher Plato in his political and legislative views. Plato maintained that only superior and divine beings, such as Kronos/Saturn, could prevent the inherent despotism of human power-bearers and thus guarantee the happiness of the human species. Kronos/Saturn is the archetype of the wise ruler, the just legislator and the magnanimous king.

After Kronos/Saturn came the divide between the gods and goddesses in the heavens and the human beings on Earth, the separation in a hierarchical social order; social classes appeared, with the fight for power and the unstable history of times of peace and wars. This is the age of iron and of bronze.

The fact that Kronos/Saturn was so ancient placed him in a position in which he did not compete with Jupiter/Zeus. He bore the title of the most ancient, wise and just god, the god of time and of Utopia, the god who reigned past any sort of conflict, who reigned in the golden age; it was for this reason that he was called to settle the conflict between the Earth (Tellus) and the heavens (Jupiter) concerning the name to be given to the human being.

There is another element that is echoed in the fable-myth of essential care; that is, the identification of Kronos/Saturn with time. In fact *khronos* with an 'h' means time in Greek. The similarity between the words 'Kronos' and *khronos* meant that the god Kronos personified time. Saturn, after being combined with Kronos, also came to symbolize time. The god Kronos/ Saturn thus assumes the same role as time: it creates everything, it yields everything and it devours everything; to him everything is submitted, he is the sovereign of the fate of people. This means that the human being becomes entangled in time, is introduced to a temporal space; the human being is a historical being who possesses a past, a present and a future, and who constructs his or her identity with the passing of time and motivated by the Utopia of integration, the golden age.

The human being is both utopian and historical-temporal. It carries within itself this dimension of Saturn and along with this the human being also carries within itself an urge towards the heavens, towards transcendence and towards the flight of the eagle (Jupiter). Finally within the human being is also revealed the weight of the Earth, of immanence, of the pecking of the chicken (Tellus).[6] It is through care that the human being keeps these powers united and makes use of them to construct his or her existence in the world and in history. It is because of this that care is essential care.

6

Dimensions of care

Now that we have enquired into the most reliable data concerning the characters of the fable-myth about care, and deciphered that which is hidden behind them, it is important for us to expand them. What is it that is hidden, in terms of life experience and of meaningfulness, behind the characters of Jupiter, Tellus and Saturn?

I have already touched on this issue, but I shall try to identify its content in detail now. It is not the case that they are autonomous beings that exist and are independent of us. It is rather the case that they exist only as metaphors which express inner dimensions of the human being, dimensions that are difficult to translate by simple conceptual language.

They also refer to centres of energy and spirituality or essential archetypes that structure life in its socio-historical fulfilment.

Others prefer to say that they are unique centres of the universal Spirit, who fills the universe with reason and purpose, and makes us humans channels for the Spirit's presence and communication within time.

At any rate, let us state something from the beginning: these spiritual energies, these centres of inner humanity, these ancient archetypes, being more metaphorical, have never lost their connection with a particular socio-historical content. They are not merely projections of our imagination without roots in reality. Nor are they simple mental matrixes as they have tended to be interpreted by some figures in the psychoanalytical tradition. In truth they are two things. These realities have their roots in ancient, communal and socio-political experiences of humanity. It is in these experiences that they have formed and been structured, and entered the collective unconscious where they live. On the other hand, they are also continuously updated as they confront new historical realities. They create a synthesis between exterior archaeology (i.e. interconnected objectivity) and interior archaeology (i.e. re-connected subjectivity). Thus it is that from this synthesis comes their great interpretative and critical importance for the present day.

In concrete and non-figurative terms, what do we mean when we speak about Jupiter, Tellus and Saturn?

Tellus: the material and earthly dimension of existence

First, let us focus on Tellus. The human being, in its various cultures and in its various historical phases, has exposed this most fundamental intuition: we belong to the Earth; we are sons and daughters of the Earth; we are Earth. As I mentioned previously, our word 'human' comes from the word *humus*. We have come from the Earth and to the Earth we shall return. The Earth is not something distinct from us. We have the Earth within us. We are Earth itself; we are Earth that in its evolutionary process has reached the stage of feeling, comprehension, will, responsibility and veneration. In short: we are Earth in its moment of self-realization and self-consciousness.

Therefore, initially there is no gap between the Earth and us. Both the Earth and we form the same complex, diverse and unique reality. This is exactly what astronauts, who were the first to contemplate the Earth from outside the Earth, witnessed. They emphatically said: from the Moon or aboard our spaceships we note no difference between the Earth and humanity, between blacks and whites, democrats and socialists, rich and poor. Humanity and Earth form a unique reality that is splendid and brilliant, and at the same time this reality is also fragile and full of vigour. This perception is not an illusion; it is entirely truthful.

In terms of modern cosmology this could be expressed as follows: we are formed by the same energies, with the same physico-chemical elements, within the same web of inter-relations that links every thing to everything and that has been in place for more than 15 billion years; a web of inter-relations that has been in place since the universe emerged in the form that we now know because of an immeasurable instability (i.e. the 'big bang' that could be equated with 'inflation and explosion'). To know about the history of the universe and of the Earth is to know about ourselves and about our ancestry.

The Cosmic Theatre

Five great acts structure the universal theatre in which we are co-actors.

The first act is the *cosmic* act. It happened in the universe as the universe expanded. To the measure that the universe expands it self-creates and self-diversifies. We were already there in the probabilities that are contained in this process of self-creation and self-diversification.

The second act is the *chemical* act. In the centre of the great red giant stars, the very first bodies to become dense, all heavy elements that today constitute each being (elements such as oxygen, carbon, silicon, nitrogen and others) were formed, and this happened at least 10 billion years ago. With the explosion of these red giants those elements spread throughout space and formed galaxies, other stars, the Earth, other planets and natural satellites that constitute the current phase of the universe. These chemical elements circulate around our whole body, blood and brains.[1]

The third act is the *biological* act. From the matter that grew increasingly more and more complex, and that unfolds itself in a process called *autopoiesis** (i.e. self-creation and self-organization*), emerged 3.8 billion years ago life in all its forms; it faced enormous threats but has always survived and has reached us in its immeasurable diversity.

The fourth act is the *human* act, a sub-chapter of the history of life. The principle of complexity and of self-creation finds in the human being immense possibilities for expansion. Human life blossomed in Africa about 10 million years ago. From there it spread out to all continents until it conquered the ends of the Earth. It showed great flexibility, it adapted to all ecosystems,* from the most icy at the poles of the Earth to the most scorching in the tropics; it adapted to the ground, to the depths of the Earth, to the air and outside of planet Earth in spaceships and on the Moon. It subdued all other remaining species and the majority of viruses and bacteria, and this was the dangerous triumph of the species *Homo sapiens* and *demens*.

Last, the fifth act is the *planetary* act. Humanity, which was divided, is uniting in its common home, the planet Earth. It discovers itself as humanity with the same origins and with the same destiny as all other beings and the Earth. It feels itself as the conscious mind of the Earth, the collective subject that is beyond particular cultures and nation-states. Through global means of communication, through the interdependence of everyone on everyone else, the global phase is emerging, a new stage in evolution. From now on history will be the history of the *Homo* species, of unified humanity and of a humanity which is interconnected with everything and with everyone.[2] We can only understand the human being-Earth if we connect it with all universal processes. In the human being-Earth, material elements and subtle energies conspired so that it was shaped and grown slowly until the moment when it could be born.

Certainly we are not the only living planet in our galaxy. It is presumed that there exist in the universe some millions of planets with conditions to sustain life, planets which are alive. Moreover, we are probably one universe side by side with other countless universes. In that case, we would be in a plural-verse rather than in a uni-verse. We would not be alone.

However, the fact that we are intelligent beings implies the convergence of certain particular conditions without which we would not be here discussing all this. Even the emergence of life requires the collaboration of certain elements that are relatively heavy, such as carbon, oxygen, nitrogen and silicon. These elements did not exist as such in the primordial soup; they were there only potentially. Only the light elements, such as hydrogen and helium, were synthesized in the universe as it originally appeared. The other elements had to wait billions of years until the great red stars appeared, in the core of which they were formed. But not all planets possess the heavy elements, the elements that are necessary for the emergence of life. Jupiter, Saturn, Uranus and Neptune, for instance, are fundamentally constituted by hydrogen and helium and as such they are inappropriate for the kind of life we know.

The Earth, within this context, presents amazing particularities. She receives an amount of solar light that is neither too weak, as in the case of Mars, nor too strong, as in the case of Venus and Mercury. She is the only planet that possesses a great quantity of water in liquid form. She shows regularity of temperatures, rhythms of evolution and sufficient stability to maintain water in its liquid state, which enable excellent conditions for the emergence of life and complex beings. If the Earth had an extremely elliptical orbit, an orbit which periodically would take us far from and then close to the Sun, or if the Earth was part of a solar system with two stars, then the existence of life would be more difficult, perhaps even impossible.

The existence of Gaia and of our own life are undoubtedly linked to the fact that our Sun provides us with medium luminosity, a Sun that is 150 million kilometres from the Earth, a Sun which is situated on the outskirts of a medium-sized spiral galaxy. This kind of existing biosphere* as well as the biological structures observed in ecosystems can only develop under very specific conditions. As a matter of fact, this means that we, understood either as Earth or as human beings, are related to the whole despite being situated in an apparently derisory corner of our galactic and universal system. The whole conspired so that we could exist and could reach this point (see *Anthropic principle* in the Glossary).

What does it mean to be Earth?

What does it really mean for us to be Earth, beyond being our ancestry, our dimension Tellus-Earth?

In the first place it means that we have Earth-elements in our bodies, blood, heart, mind and spirit. From this fact results the awareness of a deep unity.

However, we can also think about the Earth. And in so doing, we distance ourselves from her so that we can look at her better. This distancing does not break the umbilical cord that connects us to her. The fact that we have forgotten that we are connected to the Earth is the very origin of anthropocentrism, which is the illusion that because of the fact that we can think about the Earth, we have the right to set ourselves over and above her so that we can dominate her and make use of her as we wish.

Because we feel ourselves to be sons and daughters of the Earth we experience her as a generous Mother. She is a generating principle. She represents the feminine that conceives, generates and gives birth. It is in this way that the archetype Earth emerges as a Great Mother, *Pacha Mama*[3] and Nanã.[4] In the same way that she generates everything and delivers life to everything, she also welcomes and shelters everything in her bosom. When we die we return to the Mother Earth. We return to her generous and fecund womb. Feng shui,* the ecological Chinese philosophy which we will analyse later, presents death as a great sense of union with the Tao that is manifested in the energies of nature. During our lifetime we can synchronize ourselves to Tao and with the rhythms of nature so that, in truth, we escape definite death. Through death we change state so that we can return to and live in the profound mystery of nature, where all beings come from and to which all beings return.

To feel that we are Earth forces us to be down to earth. It makes us develop a new sensitivity for the Earth, her coldness and her warmth, her strength; sometimes threatening, sometimes enchanting. To feel the Earth is to feel the rain on our skin, the refreshing breeze on our face, the mighty typhoon on our body. To feel the Earth is to take a deep breath and smell the odours that enchant or repulse us. To feel the Earth is to feel her ecologic niches, it is to be connected to the spirit of each place, it is to enter a specific place, a place which one inhabits. By inhabiting it we make ourselves, in a way, prisoners of a place, of a geography, of a kind of climate, of a regime of rains and gales, of a way of living and of working and of making history. To be Earth is to be concrete, very concrete. It configures our limits. But it also stands for our solid foundations, our vantage view of the whole, our launching pad to take flight beyond this landscape and beyond this part of the Earth.

Lastly, to feel oneself Earth is to perceive oneself within a complex community with other brothers and sisters. Earth does not only generate us, human beings. She produces a myriad of microorganisms that encompass 90 per cent of the whole of the web of life; she produces insects that constitute the most important biomass of biodiversity. She produces the waters, the green cover with an infinite diversity of plants, flowers and fruits. She produces the uncountable diversity of animals, our companions within the holy unity of life, because present in all of them are the 20 amino acids that are part of the composition of life. She produces for everything the necessary conditions to subsist, to evolve and to be nourished in the ground, under the ground, in the waters and in the air. To feel oneself Earth is to dive into the community of the Earth, the world of brothers and sisters, all sons and daughters of the great and generous Mother, the Earth.

In the Palaeolithic era this understanding that we are Earth constituted the central experience of humanity. This understanding produced a form of spirituality and of politics.

Let us look first at the issue of spirituality. Beginning from Africa, some thousands of years ago, and starting specifically from the region of the Sahara when it was still a green, rich and fertile land, and passing through the Mediterranean basin, through India and China, there was a predominance of female deities, such as the Great Black Mother and the Mother Queen goddess.[5] Spirituality was seen as a profound cosmic union and an organic connection with all the elements as an expression of the Whole.

Along with this spirituality emerged, in second place, a form of politics: matriarchal institutions. Women were the organizing pillars of society and of culture. Sacred societies emerged, societies which were intertwined with reverence, emotional appeal and protection of life. To this day we carry the memory of this experience of Mother Earth in the form of archetypes and of an insatiable feeling of nostalgia for integration, which is written into our genes. Archetypes in us remind us of a real historical past which strives to be rescued and to gain validity within current life.

The human being needs to meet with this spiritual experience of organic fusion with the Earth again, with the purpose of recovering its roots and experiencing its own identity based on these roots. The human being needs also to resurrect the political memory of the feminine so that the anima dimension enters into the elaboration of policies which are more egalitarian between the sexes and which are more capable of integration.

Heavens: the spiritual and celestial
dimension of existence

The heavens are constituted by all that is above our heads: the Milky Way, myriads of stars, galaxies; in short, by deep and infinite space. Until recently the heavens were imagined to be immutable and eternal. Nowadays, with the accumulation of astronomical observations and with the use of technologies and instruments which are increasingly more sophisticated, we know that the heavens have an origin and are in constant expansion. Let us quickly glance at the history of the heavens, since it is also our history. Our spiritual and transcendent dimension is anchored in the experience of the heavens.

There is a consensus in place within the scientific community according to which everything, including the heavens, has its origins in a huge explosion (i.e. the big bang) that happened 15 billion years ago. Initially there were neither molecules, nor atoms, nor protons, nor the four fundamental interactions. There was only a formless and very concentrated soup with 10 billion degrees of heat. For no reason, this extremely dense point of energy and of original matter swelled up and exploded. It produced light and heat of an unimaginable intensity. The primordial elements were launched in all directions. There was no space within which the expansion could have occurred. Space and time themselves appeared with the great explosion, since it was the explosion that gave rise to them.

Along with the process of expansion there also occurred an increasing cooling-down process. In the measure in which it expanded, the big bang created an order of beings and relations between them, which increased in complexity and in the ability to interiorize.

To this date it is still possible to pick up the echo of that primordial explosion. Millimetrical radio waves reach us, uniformly, from all parts of the universe. It is a fossil of a pale luminosity that reminds us of the beginnings of the universe 15 billion years ago. The cooling-down process of the universe can be scientifically measured and it is currently at 3 degrees kelvin (which is about −270 degrees Celsius).

Mysteriously, only four primordial energies − gravitational force,* electromagnetic force,* weak nuclear force* and strong nuclear force* − remain unchanged. They always act synergetically and they always communicate and interact between themselves. If there had been minute alterations then the initial matter would have dispersed itself and there would never have been galaxies and stars, or the original chaos would have continued and there would never have emerged orders of complexity, such as those known by us, and we would not exist.

All these things indicate that the universe is conscious and that it possesses a purpose. If the universe wished to dream up harmony, life in its diversity and beings capable of sensibility, intelligence and love, such as us human beings, then the universe would have needed to have followed the path that it has followed.

What are these four unchangeable interactions, which give order to all universal movement, in the process of evolution and to our own vital equilibrium? We do not know. Science stays in reverent silence. But symbolic reason reckons otherwise as it believes that in these interactions we find the presence of the Great Spirit, of God the Creator in continuous activity. The Great Spirit expresses its Grandeur, reveals its Wisdom and demonstrates its Love in the whole and in each one of its parts through the joined interaction of these four fundamental energies, true laws of nature. If we know the laws, why not recognize the supreme Legislator?

When we refer to the heavens, we describe this incommensurable and mysterious reality. It exceeds our capacities. It transcends our ability to reach it. And, despite all this, we always want to reach it. Our desire is to cross infinite space and reach the ends of the heavens. Certainly it is so because we keep the ancestral memory of our heavenly origins. Although we are rooted on Earth, we have our mind anchored in the heavens.

We have the heavens within us. This represents the heavenly dimension of the transcendence of the human being, the human capacity to go beyond the limits of the Earth, and human beings' untiring efforts always to ascend and to reach higher and higher. It can also be interpreted as the rise of the masculine principle, providing order, the explorer of new horizons, a wanderer insatiable in the face of all that is within the reach of its hands.

The uranic (heaven) experience also generated, as did the telluric (Earth) experience, a form of spirituality and of politics. This form of spirituality is based on the rupture of the roots, an infinite openness and a continuous search for new visions. This spirituality, in its extreme form, is structured in dualism: heavens–Earth, above–below, this world–the other world, desire–realization. It is particular to the masculine to make this separation and to live this dualism. Duality exists and reveals the complexities of the real. Dualism is different from duality. Dualism considers things to be apart, while duality sees things together, as dimensions of the same and unique reality. Instrumental and analytic reason presupposes this dualistic separation and inaugurates a division, which is false, between the subject and the object, the I and the world, the feminine and the masculine. It tries to turn everything into an object of desire, conquest, possession and appropriation. It conflicts with our telluric experience of a vital connection of every thing with everything, within the great Whole.

During the Neolithic period, masculine values started to predominate and a new form of politics was founded. Men assumed a position of power in society. They instigated patriarchalism with the submission of women and the domination of nature. The loss of the re-connection of every thing with everything is a result of patriarchal culture that did not integrate the previous contributions of matriarchalism. This loss underlies our current main political institutions and religions. And it shows its dangerous limits through the carelessness that it shows towards the planet Earth, through the lack of care towards life in all its forms and in the increase of conflicts in social relations.

How are we to search for a synthesis between the heavenly dimension (Jupiter) and the earthly dimension (Tellus)? How are we to bring together our wish to take roots in our common home, the Earth, with our insatiable desire for the infinite, the heavens? This is the central tension in the human being; it is an extreme anthropological challenge. The evocation of Saturn will show us the way.

History and Utopia: the fundamental human condition

The mythological figure of Saturn represents the archetype of synthesis, the golden age, the realization of the Utopia of those who have been redeemed and freed at home and in the fatherland and motherland of complete identity. In the kingdom of Saturn, gods and men and women lived together in absolute integration, in justice, in benevolence and in complete peace. It is Utopia. But is it just Utopia?

We have established that the human being and society cannot live without some form of Utopia. That is to say, the human being and society can neither stop projecting their best dreams nor can they give up on the search for these dreams day after day. If there were no Utopias then minor interests would prevail. Everybody would wallow in the swamp of a history without hope because it would always be dominated by the stronger ones. The dimension of Saturn, Utopia, on the contrary always creates new perspectives and continuously finds a thousand reasons to fight and to search for better ways of living together. Utopia is the presence of the heavenly dimension within the earthly dimension, within the strict limits of personal and collective existence.

However, Utopia cannot be utopian. If it were so then it would become pure fantasy and an irresponsible escape from reality. Utopia must fulfil itself within a historical process that tries to give body to the dream and build up, step by step, the thousand paces that are necessary for the pathway. History requires time, patience, expectation, the overcoming of obstacles, and work to build it up. It is the earthly dimension making its demands on human existence.

The human being lives stretched between Utopia and history. The human being is in the point of time where Utopia and history meet. It is not without reason that Saturn also expressed the rule of time with his sovereignty. The human being constructs its own existence within time. It requires time to grow up, learn, mature, gain wisdom and even to die. Within time it lives the tension between the Utopia that livens it up whenever it looks up and forward, and real history that forces it to find compromises, to take concrete steps and to look attentively at the pathway and its direction, its forking out, its obstacles, its traps and chances.

It is in history, built by the forces of Utopia, that the synthesis between the demands of the Earth and the imperatives of the heavens is elaborated. It is in history that the opportunity for a total experience of connection with the Whole (feminine principle) and at the same time for a continuous openness towards the infinite (masculine principle) is created. Ultimately, we are an infinite project. And the infinite unbalances any sort of synthesis. It forces us to comprehend our condition as an open system that is able to incorporate the new and is always capable of creating new synthesis.

How do we make visible this synthesis between heavens–Earth, Utopia–history? How do we keep it alive, fecund and always attractive? It is here that we evoke Care. The fable-myth of Hyginus teaches us through the mouth of the god Saturn that Care accompanies the human being while it makes its pilgrimage through time. Care is the utopian-historic pathway of the synthesis that is possible to us, finite beings. It is for this reason that Care is the fundamental ethos, the deciphering key, of the human being and of its potential.

7

The nature of care

We have just completed a voyage through pivotal human
experiences that lay hidden beneath the fable-myth of Hyginus
with its respective basic concepts. We have left behind a char-
acterization of Care. Now it is time to go deeper into its
nature. In Hyginus, Care is not seen as a deity, rather it is seen
as a personification of a fundamental way-of-being. However,
this personification is equivalent to turning Care divine; divine
in the sense of what we attribute to mythological deities as beings
expressing basic human dimensions.

It is important here for us to look at the phenomenology
of care. By phenomenology I mean the way in which any reality becomes a phenomenon for our conscience, shows itself
in our experiences and gives shape to our practices. In this
sense it is not a case of thinking or talking about care as an
object independent of us; it is rather to think and to talk
starting with care as it is lived and as it structures ourselves.
We do not *have* care. We *are* care. This means that care possesses an ontological dimension that is part of the human
constitution. It is a way-of-being unique to men and women.
Without care we are no longer human beings.

In *Being and Time*, Martin Heidegger (1889–1976), par
excellence the philosopher of care, showed that realities as
fundamental as wants and desires are found to be rooted in
essential care. Only from the dimension of care can these
emerge as human realizations. Care is, as Heidegger says, an
'ontological constitution' always underlying

man's *perfectio* – his transformation into that which he can be in Being free for his outmost possibilities (projection) – is 'accomplished' by 'care' . . . the phenomenon of care and of all fundamental *existentialia* is . . . broad enough to present a basis . . . [for] . . . *every* interpretation of Dasein [of the human being].[1]

By 'ontological constitution' Heidegger understands that which enters into the essential definition of the human being and that structures a human being's practices. When he talks about care as 'a basis . . . [for] . . . *every* interpretation of Dasein [of the human being]' he signals that care is fundamental to any interpretation of the human being.[2] If we do not refer to care we cannot achieve an understanding of the human being. This is exactly what I have been asserting throughout my reflections thus far, and it is appropriate for me now to take it further.

The philology of the word 'care'

Perhaps the first approach to the core meaning of care is found in its philology. As philosophers have pointed out, words are loaded with existential meanings. In words, human beings have accumulated an infinite number of experiences, which have been positive and negative; experiences of searching, of meeting, of certainty, of bewilderment and of immersing ourselves in Being. We must draw out from words their hidden richness. Usually a word is created within a niche and with an original meaning, and from that moment onwards it unfolds itself assuming different meanings. This seems to be the case with the origins of the word 'care'.

According to classic dictionaries of philology some scholars have derived the word 'care' from the Latin *cura*.[3] The word *cura* is the scholarly synonym of the word 'care', and it is present in Martin Heidegger's *Being and Time* when he gives

the original text of the fable-myth of Care. In its most ancient form, *cura* in Latin was written as *coera* and it was used
within the context of relations of love and friendship. It expressed the attitude of care, of devotion, of concern and of
worry for the loved one or for a favourite object.

Another school of thought has derived the word care from
cogitare-cogitatus and its corruptions *coyedar*, *coidar* and
cuidar. The meaning of *cogitare-cogitatus* is the same as that of
cura: to contemplate, to think, to bring to attention, to show
interest, to reveal an attitude of devotion and of concern.
Care can emerge only when the existence of someone has
importance for me. From that moment I continue to dedicate
myself to this person; I am willing to take part in this person's
destiny, this person's searches, sufferings, successes; in short,
I am willing to take part in this person's life.

Care thus means devotion, commitment, diligence, zeal,
attention and good treatment. As I have said, we have here a
fundamental attitude, a way of being through which a person
comes out of itself and centres itself in the other with devotion and commitment. We know in the Latin languages the
expression *cura d'almas* (the cure of souls), which designates
a priest or a pastor whose mission is to care for the spiritual
well-being of people and to accompany them in their religious
path. This work is done with care and *esprit de finesse* as it is
appropriate to spiritual issues.

The attitude of care can lead to preoccupation, concern and
a feeling of responsibility. Thus, for instance, we say in
Portuguese: 'This child is all my care (preoccupation).' Padre
Antônio Vieira, a classic writer of the Portuguese language, wrote:
'These are, friend, all of my cares (my concerns).'[4] An ancient
adage preached: 'Those who have cares do not sleep.' The
Latins knew the expression *dolor amoris* (love's pain) to express
the *cura*, the anxiety and the care for the loved one. Another
example is: 'I handed my son over to the care of the school's
headmaster (I have put my son under his responsibility).'

Because of its own nature, care includes two basic senses which are closely interlinked. The first sense is the attitude of devotion, of commitment and of paying attention to the other. The second sense is that of preoccupation and concern because the person who has care feels involved and emotionally linked to the other.

With good reason the great Latin poet Horace (65–8 BCE) could finally observe: 'Care is the permanent companion of the human being.' That is to say: care always accompanies the human being because the human being will never stop loving and devoting itself to someone (first sense), nor will the human being stop preoccupying and concerning itself for the loved one (second sense). If it was not like this then the human being would not feel involved with the other person and would show negligence and carelessness for its own life and destiny. Ultimately, it would reveal indifference, which represents the death of love and of care.

Two ways of being-in-the-world: work and love

The two basic meanings yielded from the philological analysis confirm the idea that care is more than a particular act or a virtue alongside others. Care is a way of being; that is, it is the way through which the human being structures itself and through which it interacts with others in the world. In other words: it is a way of being-in-the-world in which the relations that are established with all things are founded.

When we say 'being-in-the-world' we are not expressing a geographical point such as being in nature, close to plants, animals and other human beings. This notion can be part of it, but an understanding of being-in-the-world is something more encompassing. It means a way of existing and of co-existing, a way of being present, of navigating through reality and of relating to all things in the world. In this co-existence and in this living together, in this navigation and in this play of relations, the human being builds its own being, its self-consciousness, and its own identity.

At the most fundamental level, there are two basic ways of being-in-the-world: work and care. It is here that the process of construction of human reality emerges.

The way-of-being through work

The way-of-being-in-the-world through work appears in the form of interaction and intervention. The human being does not live in a biological *siesta* with nature. On the contrary, the human being interacts in nature, seeks nature's laws and rhythms, and also intervenes with nature to make its own life more comfortable. It is through work that the human being does this. Through work the human being builds its own 'habitat', it adapts the environment to its desires and matches its desires to the environment. Through work it extends evolution and it introduces realities that evolution would possibly never produce, such as a building, a city, a car, and means of communication such as the radio and the television. Through work the human being acts as a co-pilot to the evolutionary process, it makes nature and society with its organizations, systems and technological apparatus enter into symbioses* and co-evolve* together.

In a way, work is present in the dynamics of nature itself. Plants or animals also work to the extent that they interact with their environment, exchange information, show themselves to be flexible and adapt in order to survive. In the human being, however, work is transformed into a conscious way-of-being and takes on the character of a project and a strategy with its tactics of moulding the human being itself and nature.

Originally, work was more to do with interaction than with intervention since the human being had an attitude of veneration towards nature. The human being only used what it required to survive and to make its existence more secure and enjoyable.

The process of intervention in nature started with *Homo habilis* between 2 and 1.6 million years ago when the first tools were invented. And intervention became a constant with *Homo sapiens*, from which we descend directly, 150,000 years ago. It became an organic process in the Neolithic, 10,000 years ago, when the human being started building dwellings and towns, and domesticating plants and animals, a process that culminated in the techno-science of our day.

It was through work that human beings formed cultures as a way of shaping themselves and nature. In this way the path leading to the hunger for power over and domination of nature was open. This hunger and domination reinvigorates itself when the human being feels challenged by the obstacles that it faces. The human being increased its aggressiveness and greatly increased its industry and ingenuity. It started to use instrumental and analytic reasoning, which is much more effective for a profound intervention in nature. This kind of reasoning requires *objectivity* as it imposes a certain distancing from reality so that it is able to study this reality as an object with the aim of accumulating experiences, and of taking possession of reality.

It is appropriate here to emphasize that the *objects* are not objects per se. They are turned into objects by rationality since it isolates these objects from their respective environments, it separates them from their existential companions and it uses them for its own interests. Objectivity is a projection of rationality. The said objects, in truth, are subjects that have a history; they have accumulated and exchanged information and they belong to the cosmic and terrestrial community.

As the human being advanced in its efforts to objectify and to give form to the objects of its thoughts, it created apparatuses that helped it to save its energies and that increased the power of its senses. Currently, an increasing number of tasks are done by machines, computers, automata and robots that substitute, by and large, for the human workforce. Now has emerged something that has been conventionally called a cybiont:* a hybrid superorganism, made up of human beings, machines and webs of information. In this way the connection between the biological, the mechanical and the electronic, which constitutes the basis of our modern societies, has been made.

The logic of being-in-the-world within the mode of work represents one's positioning *over* things so that one can dominate these things and put them to the service of personal and collective interests. The human being is placed in the centre of everything, which is called anthropocentrism. Anthropocentrism describes an attitude that is centred in the human being and in which things have meaning only to the extent to which they are related to the human being and satisfy a human being's desire. It negates the autonomy that things possess. Moreover, it forgets the connection that the human being itself has, whether it likes it or not, with nature and with all realities since the human being is part of the whole. Lastly, anthropocentrism ignores the fact that the ultimate subject of life, of sensitivity, of intelligence and of love is not primarily us, but the universe itself, especially the Earth. The Earth manifests its capacity to feel, to think, to love and to venerate through us and in us. Anthropocentrism does not recognize all these overlapping points.

This attitude of work-power over the world embodies the dimension of the masculine in men and women. It is the dimension that compartmentalizes reality in order to know more fully and conquer reality; it uses power and even aggression to reach its utilitarian objectives; it launches itself outside itself in the adventure of knowledge and in the conquest of all places of the Earth and, in modern times, in the conquest of outer and celestial space. The masculine dimension started to dominate from the Neolithic and currently it has reached its zenith with the occupation and humanization of the whole planet.

The way-of-being through care

The other way of being-in-the-world is realized through care. Care is not in opposition to work; rather it gives work a different shade. Through care we do not see nature and everything that exists in nature as objects. Through care the relation is not subject–object, but subject–subject. We experience entities as subjects, as values, as symbols that bear a connection to a foundational Reality. Nature is not mute. It speaks and evokes. It emits messages of grandeur, beauty, complexity and power. The human being can listen and interpret these signals. The human being can put itself close to things, *together* with things, and feel united to them. The human being does not just exist; it co-exists with everything else. The relationship is not one of establishing domination *over*; it is rather a relationship of living together. It is not sheer intervention; it is rather interaction and communion.

To take care of things implies having intimacy, feeling these things inside, welcoming and sheltering them, and giving these things rest and peace. To take care is to enter into synchronicity with them; it is to listen to their rhythm and to tune oneself into this rhythm. Analytic-instrumental reasoning gives way to cordial reasoning, to the *esprit de finesse*, the spirit of kindness, the profound feeling. Centre stage is no longer occupied by logos* rationality; it is rather occupied by pathos* sentiment.

This way of being-in-the-world, in the form of care, allows the human being to live the fundamental experience of value, of that which has importance and fundamentally counts. This is not the utilitarian value that is based only on a thing's usefulness, but is the intrinsic value that things have. From this substantive value emerge the dimensions of otherness, of respect, of sacredness, of reciprocity and of complementarity.

We all feel ourselves connected and re-connected to each other, forming an organic and unique whole that is diverse and always inclusive. This whole has an ultimate Link that reconnects, supports and animates everything. This Link emerges as a supreme Value which hides itself and reveals itself in everything. It has the character of Mystery, in the sense that it always announces itself and always conceals itself. This Mystery does not cause fear; it fascinates and attracts like a sun. It lets itself be experienced as a great welcoming Womb that fulfils us completely. It is also called God.

Within the way-of-being through care, resistance occurs and bewilderment emerges. But these are overcome by persistent patience. In the place of aggressiveness, there is living together in love. Instead of domination, there is affectionate companionship alongside and together with the other.

The way-of-being through care reveals the feminine dimension in men and women. The feminine has always been present in history. But in the Palaeolithic it gained historical visibility when cultures were matrifocal* and people lived in ways integrated with nature. People felt themselves incorporated in the whole. These were societies marked by a profound sense of the sacredness of the universe, and by a reverence in the face of the mysteriousness of life and of the Earth. Women held historic and social power and gave the feminine an expression so profound that it stayed in the permanent memory of humankind through its great symbols, dreams and archetypes that are present in culture and in collective consciousness.

The dictatorship of the way-of-being through work

The great challenge for the human being is to combine work with care. They do not oppose themselves; they compose themselves. They put a limit on each other and at the same time they complete each other. Together they constitute the wholeness of human experience, which is on the one hand linked to materialism, and on the other is linked to spirituality. The mistake consists in seeing one dimension opposing the other and not seeing that these dimensions are ways-of-being of the unique and same human being.

Since the most ancient of times we have witnessed a drama of perverse consequences: the rupture between work and care. From the Neolithic period, 10,000 years ago, work gradually came to predominate as a frenetic search for efficiency, a hectic effort to produce and an unconstrained yearning for the subjugation of the Earth. The last centuries, however, especially with the industrialization process that started in the eighteenth century, have been characterized by the dictatorship of the way-of-being through work as intervention, production and domination. Work is no longer related to nature (in the form of giving shape or moulding); it is rather related to economic capital (this is the confrontation between work and capital which was argued by Marx and Engels). Work is now for wages and is no longer an activity of merging with nature. People live enslaved by the structures of productive, rationalized, objectified and depersonalized work; they are submitted to the rationale of the machines.

A fine Colombian commentator, Luis Carlos Restrepo, has said, with reason, that we have all made ourselves heirs of Alexander the Great (356–323 BCE), the archetype of the warrior and conqueror. Alas, the latent ideology of the way-of-being through work-domination is the conquest of the other, of the world, of nature, in the form of a simple and complete subjugation, as was the way of Alexander.

For this reason, the dictatorship of the way-of-being through work-domination has masculinized relations. It opened the way to anthropocentrism, to androcentrism,* to patriarchalism and to machismo. We are tied up with pathological expressions of the masculine that are disconnected from the feminine; the animus over the anima.

Care has been slandered as a feminization of human practices, as an impediment to objectivity in the understanding, and as an obstacle to efficiency.

The dictatorship of the way-of-being through work-domination is currently taking humanity to a decisive deadlock: either we put limits to productivist voracity by associating work and care, or we are going to encounter the worst. Through the great increase of productive work the non-renewable resources of the Earth have been exhausted and the physico-chemical balance of the Earth has been broken. Sociability between humans has been torn apart by the domination of some peoples by others and by the hard-fought battle of the classes. We see nothing else in the human being apart from its work-power, which is to be sold and explored for its capacity for production and consumption. An increasing number of people, in reality two-thirds of humanity, have been condemned to a life without any form of sustainability. We have lost the notion of the human being as a being-of-relations, unlimited relations, a being of creativity, tenderness, care, spirituality and carrier of a sacred and infinite project.

The way-of-being-in-the-world based exclusively on work can destroy the planet. Thus the current urgency in rescuing the way-of-being through care with its essential corrective. In this way the emergence of the cybiont is possible, a being that enters into symbiosis with a machine, not in order to be submitted to the machine, but in order to better its own life and environment.

The recovery of the way-of-being through care

The recovery of the way-of-being through care is not achieved to the detriment of work; it is rather done through a different way of understanding and performing work. In order to do this the human being needs to turn itself to itself and discover its way-of-being through care.

Let us take up again our reflections about the nature of essential care. The entry point cannot be calculatory, analytic and objective rationality. This would take us to work-intervention-production and there it would imprison us. Machines and computers are more efficient than we are in the use of this kind of rationality-work.

There is something in human beings that is not found in machines; something which appeared millions of years ago in the evolutionary process when mammals emerged, a class of which we are part: this is sentiment, the capacity of emotion, the capacity to involve oneself, the capacity to affect and to be affected.

Computers and robots do not have the character to take care of the environment, or cry for the misfortunes of others, or rejoice in the happiness of a friend. A computer does not have a heart.

Only we human beings can sit at the table with a frustrated friend, put our hand on his shoulder, drink a pint of beer with him and bring consolation and hope to him. We build the world starting with bonds of affection. These bonds make people and situations precious, loaded with value. We are preoccupied with them. We take time to dedicate ourselves to them. We feel responsible for the bond that has grown between us and others. The category of care encompasses all these ways of being. It shows how we function as human beings.

It is here that we find the evidence that the original fact is not the logos, rationality and the structures of understanding, but the pathos, sentiment, the capacity for sympathy and empathy, dedication, care and communion with the other. Everything starts with feeling. Feeling is that which makes us sensitive to what is around us; it is that which makes us like and dislike. It is feeling that unites us with things and that gets us involved with people. It is feeling that produces enchantment in the face of the grandeur of the heavens, or veneration before the grandeur of Mother Earth, and that nurtures emotions in the face of the fragility of a newborn child.

Let us remind ourselves here of a phrase from *The Little Prince* by Antoine de Saint Exupéry, a phrase which was very successful in captivating the collective unconscious of millions of readers: 'It is only with the heart that one can see rightly; what is essential is invisible to the eye'.[5] It is feeling that makes people, things and situations important to us. This profound feeling, I repeat, is called 'care'. Only something which has aroused emotion, that evoked a profound feeling and that provoked care, leaves indelible marks and remains for good.

Modern thinking has rescued the centrality of feeling, the importance of tenderness, of compassion and of care, especially through the deep psychology of Freud, Jung, Adler, Rogers and Hillman, and currently through genetics and the anthropological implications of quantum physics* through Niels Bohr (1885–1962) and Werner Heisenberg (1901–76).

More than the Cartesian *cogito ergo sum*, I think therefore I am, is the *sentio ergo sum*, I feel therefore I am. The book by Daniel Goleman, *Emotional Intelligence*, has become an international best-seller because, through the use of empirical investigations of the brain and neurology, it demonstrated what Plato (427–347 BCE), St Augustine (354–450 CE), the medieval Franciscan school of St Bonaventura and Duns Scotus in the thirteenth century, Pascal (1623–62 CE), Schleiermacher (1768–1834 CE) and Heidegger had already taught. That is, the basic dynamic of the human being is pathos, it is feeling, it is care, it is the logic of the heart. 'Rational mind', asserts Goleman, 'takes one or two moments longer to register and react than emotional mind; the first impulse . . . is of the heart, not of the head.'[6]

We are now in a better position to understand, in depth, the fable-myth of Hyginus about Care. Care is so essential that it is prior to the spirit infused by Jupiter and the body furnished by Earth. Therefore, the concept of the human being as a composite of spirit and body is not the original one. The fable says that 'Care first shaped this creature (the human being)'. Care is found beforehand, it is ontologically a priori, it is at the origins of the human being. This origin is not only a temporal beginning. It has a philosophical sense of a fountain that permanently springs with being. Therefore, this means that care constitutes, in human existence, an energy that uninterruptedly gushes out at each moment and in every circumstance. Care is the original force that continuously gives rise to the human being. Without care, the human being would continue to be only a lump of clay like any other in the banks of a river, or a disembodied angelic spirit outside historic time.

It was carefully that Care shaped the human being. And in doing so Care exerted dedication, tenderness, devotion, feeling and heart. And as such it created responsibilities and gave rise to a preoccupation with the being it had created. These dimensions, true constituting principles, became part of the composition of the human being. They became flesh and blood. Without these dimensions the human being would never be a human being. For this reason, the fable-myth of Hyginus ends up emphasizing that care will accompany the human being through its life, through its temporal journey in the world.

A psychoanalyst who is attentive to the drama faced by modern civilization, such as the North American Rollo May, could well have commented:

> Our situation is the following: in the current confusion of rationalist and technical episodes we have lost the sight of, and become unpreoccupied with, the human being; we must humbly go back to simple care now . . . the myth of care – and I believe, very often, it is only it – that allows us to resist cynicism and apathy that are the psychological diseases of our times.

What our civilization needs is to overcome the dictatorship of the way-of-being through work-production-domination. This dictatorship keeps us hostages of a logic that today is shown to be destructive to the Earth and to its resources, to relations between peoples, to interactions between work and economic capital, to spirituality and to our sense of belonging to a common destiny. Freed from exhausting and dehumanizing work, now done by automatic machines, we could recover the notion of work in its original anthropological sense, as a merger with nature and as a creative activity, work that is able to fulfil the human being and to construct meanings that are increasingly more integrated with the dynamics of nature and of the universe.

It is important to put care into everything. For this we must develop the anima that is within us. This means granting rights of citizenship to our capacity of feeling the other; empathy towards all beings who suffer, human or non-human; obeying more the logic of the heart, of cordiality, of kindness than the logic of conquest and of the utilitarian use of things.

To give centrality to care does not mean stopping working and intervening in the world. It means renouncing the hunger for power that reduces everything to objects that are disconnected from human subjectivity. It means imposing limits on the obsession with efficacy at any cost. It means bringing down the dictatorship of cold and abstract rationality and giving space to care. It means organizing work in synchronicity with nature and its rhythms and manifestations. It means respecting the communion which all things have with each other and with us. It means putting the collective interest of society, of the whole biotic and earthly community, above the interests that are exclusively human. It means coming close to each thing that one wishes to transform so that this thing does not suffer, is not uprooted from its habitat, and is able to maintain the conditions for its development and co-evolve together with its ecosystems and with Earth itself. It means picking up the presence of the Spirit beyond our human limits in the universe, in plants, in living organisms, in the great simian gorillas, chimpanzees and orang-utans, who are also bearers of feeling, language and cultural habits similar to ours.

These are the antidotes to the abandonment that the poor and elderly feel. This is the medicine against the lack of care which the excluded, unemployed, retired, elderly and youngsters denounce in the majority of public institutions. These institutions are increasingly less concerned with the human being and are more preoccupied with the economy, the stock market, interest rates, and the unlimited growth of goods and material services, which is appropriate to the privileged classes but to the detriment of the dignity and compassion that are required in the face of the needs of the great majority. This is the remedy that will be able to put a stop to the devastation of the biosphere and to the compromising of the fragile balance of Gaia. This is the way-of-being that rescues our most essential humanity.

8

Resonances of care

Care as a way-of-being is intertwined with all human existence and it possesses resonances in various important human attitudes. Through care the heavenly dimensions (transcendence) and the earthly dimensions (immanence) find their equilibrium and co-existence. Care also takes place in the kingdom of living beings since every life needs care because otherwise it falls ill and dies. It is interesting to mention here the case of the *tucunaré*, one of our best-liked fish. Father and mother take great care of their offspring (*alevins*). They make their nest by digging a hole in the bottom of the river and they swim around it in order to protect their offspring. When their offspring try leaving the nest, the parents accompany them and alert them against spreading out. In response to minimum threat the offspring return all together to their nest, guided by the parents. Stragglers are carefully collected into the mouths of the parents and returned to the group.

I wish to list here some of the resonances of care. These are related concepts that are derived from innermost care and that translate care in different concrete forms. I have here highlighted the following seven: love as a biological phenomenon; the right measure; tenderness; caress; cordiality; conviviality; and compassion. One could also add synergy, hospitality, courtesy and kindness. These, however, are implicit within those I will address.

Love as a biological phenomenon

Love is one of the most trivialized words in our speech, and as an interpersonal phenomenon is one of the most corrupted. I shall broach the subject of love within the fecund perspective of one of the most prominent modern biologists, the Chilean Humberto Maturana. In his reflections love is thought of as a biological phenomenon. Love happens within the dynamics of life, from life's most primary occurrences, billions and billions of years ago, to its greatest complexities at the level of the human being. Let us inquire how love is introduced into the universe.

Within nature there are two kinds of coupling of beings with their environment; one is necessary, the other spontaneous. The former, the necessary, causes all beings to be interconnected one with the other and linked to their respective ecosystems as a guarantee of survival. There is, however, another kind of coupling that happens spontaneously. Some beings interact without survival reasons; they interact by pure pleasure within the flow of their lives. This is about dynamic and reciprocal unions between living beings and organic systems. There are no reasons for these unions. They happen because they happen. This is an original event of life in its sheer spontaneity.

When one welcomes the other and thus co-existence happens, love emerges as a biological phenomenon. This phenomenon tends to expand itself and to gain more complex forms. One of these forms is the human, which is more than simply spontaneous as in the case of all other living beings; in the human form, it rather becomes a project of freedom that conscientiously welcomes the other and creates the conditions for establishing love as the highest value of life.

Within this tendency emerges an enlarged love which is socialization; love is the basis of the social phenomenon and not a consequence of it. In other words, it is love that gives origin to society; society exists because there is love and not for the opposite reason as is commonly believed. If there is a lack of love (the basis) the social is destroyed. If, nevertheless, the social perseveres it gains the form of an organization that has been forced together, an aggregation of domination and violence of one against the other, one coercing the other. For this reason whenever the union and the congruence between beings is destroyed, love is also destroyed, and if there is destruction of love then social relations are also destroyed. Love is always an opening to the other, a living together and a communion with the other.

It was not the fight for survival of the strongest that guaranteed the perseverance of life and of individuals; it was rather the cooperation and the co-existence between them. Hominids* millions of years ago became human beings proportionately as they increased sharing among themselves the results of their gathering and hunting, and sharing with others their affections. Language itself, which so characterizes the human being, emerged within this dynamism of love and sharing.

Competition, emphasizes Humberto Maturana, is antisocial, both today and long ago, because it implies the negation of the other and the refusal to share and to love. Modern neoliberal society, especially the market society, rests on competition. This is what makes modern societies exclusive, inhuman and capable of producing many victims. This competitive logic prevents modern society from being a bearer of happiness and offering a future for humanity and for the Earth.

How is human love characterized? Maturana answers: 'What is especially human in love is not love, but that which we do in love while humans ... it is our particular way of living together as social beings in speech ... without love we are not social beings.'[1]

Love is a cosmic and biological phenomenon. When it reaches the level of the human it reveals itself with powerful aggregation, sympathy and solidarity. People unite themselves and recreate through the use of the language of love the feeling of affection and of belonging to the same destiny and to the same historic pathway.

Without essential care, love does not happen, it is not maintained, it does not expand itself, and it does not allow for association between beings. Without care there are no proper conditions that might favour the flourishing of that which truly humanizes: deep feeling, willingness to share and the search for love.

The golden rule: the right measure

In the last chapter I dealt with the question of the right measure between the way-of-being in the world through work and the way-of-being in the world through care, and it was established that there is a great imbalance in culture since it has been globalized under the auspices of the dictatorship of the way-of-being through work. The question here is: How much care must we incorporate in order to be able to rescue the lost balance? This is a crucial question for theory and for practice.

Let us first make an observation here: the meaning of measurement is found in many fields from geometry to religion. But it is within the subject of ethics that the right measure assumes pivotal importance. It is about finding the *optimum relative*, the equilibrium between excess and deficiency.

On the one hand, measure is felt negatively as a limit to our aspirations. From this emerges the desire to go and even the pleasure in going beyond the limit and trespassing into the forbidden. On the other hand, it is felt positively as the capacity to use, in a moderate way, natural, social and personal potentialities so that these last longer and are able to reproduce themselves. This is only possible when a certain balance and the right measure is established. The right measure is achieved by realistic recognition, by humble acceptance and by the best use of limitations, by conferring sustainability on all phenomena and processes, on the Earth, on societies and on people.

This search for the right measure was particularly strong in the cultures of the Mediterranean basin, especially for the Egyptians, Greco-Latins and Hebrews. It is sometimes said that the context of the culture of measure is also the context of the culture of excesses because within this context we find the elaboration of the most extreme ideologies and wars without any form of restraint. This search is of central concern in Buddhism and in the ecological philosophy of Chinese feng shui. For all these the symbols are scales and respective feminine deities, who are the guardians of equilibrium.

The search for measure is surrounded by difficult questions that should not be disregarded, questions such as:

- What is the right measure?
- Who establishes the right measure?
- From which sources of knowledge is the right measure established?
- Is the measure always dependent on cultures, different historical situations, personal and collective human subjectivity?

I will not attempt to answer all these questions as this would be very lengthy. I will, however, attempt an argument which sufficiently encompasses them.

Many were the pathways attempted in establishing the right measure. Usually these pathways were centred around a particular pillar: it either derives solely from nature; or solely from universal rationality; or uniquely in empirical sciences; or solely from the wisdom of the peoples; or uniquely from the wisdom of religions; or solely from the divine revelation contained in the sacred texts of the Judaeo-Christian tradition, of the Upanishad* and of Taoism.*

Nowadays we are increasingly convinced that nothing can be reduced to a single cause (monocausality) or to one single factor, since nothing is linear and simple. Everything is complex and woven in inter-retro-relations and webs of inclusiveness. Like pillars which support a bridge, anything may lead us to more integrating solutions because each thing is able to shed some light and communicate some truth on the matter. Wisdom is being able to see each part within an articulated whole, which can be exemplified by the beautiful figure of a mosaic that is made of thousands of tesserae, or an amazing lacework made of a thousand colourful threads.

The right measure and nature

By 'nature' I mean the collection of organic and inorganic entities, energies and energetic and morphogenic* fields that exist as organized systems within other larger systems, which may or may not be affected by human intervention, and which constitute a whole that is organic, dynamic and in search of equilibrium. The human being is part and parcel of nature, and maintains with nature a sophisticated web of relations that makes the human being co-pilot of the evolutionary process along with the guiding forces of nature.

Nature is a reality that is so complex and vast that it cannot be encapsulated by any definition. What nature is in itself remains a mystery, and as mystery it is being and nothingness. What we possess are cultural discourses about nature by the ancients, by Hinduism* in India, by Taoism in China, by Zen Buddhism* in Japan, by modern Copernican science, by quantum mechanics, by the theory of open systems, by genetic and molecular biology, and by the new cosmology based on the sciences of the Earth. My understanding is very indebted to these traditions, especially to the last one. Within the function of each understanding it is decided which kind of nature is to be preserved.

When we contemplate nature, despite chaotic expressions and very intricate complexities, it is obvious that there is an immanent measure that is not the result of the parts taken in isolation but the result of the organic and living whole. There is harmony and equilibrium. Nature is not bio-centred, it is not centred in life only, but in the dynamic balance between life and death.

For contemporary scholars, nature is the result of an immense evolutionary process that goes beyond the model of Charles Darwin (1809–82), which was fundamentally restricted to the biosphere. The current understanding, which is called 'the synthetic theory of evolution', understands evolution as a universal theory: from the big bang everything in the universe is evolving. This process is not linear, it jumps and experiences fluctuations* and bifurcations. It is not merely expanding but creating new possibilities. All this means that the laws of nature do not possess a deterministic character but a probabilistic one.

Our knowledge of thermodynamics* demonstrates that life and any novelty in the universe emerges from a certain distance and from a certain rupture of equilibrium. This absence of measure, in spite of being momentary, provokes the self-organization (autopoiesis) that creates a new stability and a new dynamic balance. It is dynamic because it continuously reinvents itself, and it does so not by the reproduction of the previous equilibrium, but by the creation of a new one through dialogue with the environment and a new adaptation. The logic of nature in the evolutionary process is the following: organization, break of organization, disorganization, new relation, new equilibrium, new organization. It is permanently like this.

This does not mean that nature does not have a measure (laws of nature); nature possesses a measure that is not static and mechanical, but dynamic and fluctuating, characterized by constants and variations. There are phases of rupture, and soon after that the gestation of a new regularity. The climate of the Earth, for instance, during its 3.8 billion years of existence, has gone through turbulences and terrible devastations.

The Earth has already been almost twice as warm as it is today and, despite this, has shown along this 3.8 billion-year time-line an incredible dynamic equilibrium that has benevolently favoured all forms of life.

Seeing nature as a whole does not impose precepts. It points out tendencies and regularities that can go in various directions. It is up to the human being to develop sensitivity in order to catch these tendencies and make decisions. Nature does not excuse the human being from deciding and from exercising freedom. Only thus can the human being show itself to be an ethical being.

This space for intervention and for creation that the conscious and responsible human being has is a gift from nature. Just as nature continuously and dynamically searches, invents and reinvents its measure, in the same way the human being must search for the right measure, not once and for all, but always paying attention to what is occurring in nature, in history, and within itself. The right measure changes. What does not change is the constant search for the right measure.

There is also the issue of the global process that shows an arrow of time always pointing forward and upwards, and the more the process advances the less it replicates itself, the less it clones itself and the more diversity it presents. The measures may vary but each measure that is found serves as a superior purpose that takes forward the arrow of evolution.

The right measure and pathos

How does the human being catch this multidimensional measure of nature? Rational knowledge is not enough, nor is the obedient will enough to identify regularities, nor doing without human creativity and the exercise of freedom that are particular to the human being. It is important to develop an attentive attitude to listening, a profound sentiment of iden-tification with nature, with its changes and stabilities. The human being must feel itself to be nature. The more the human being immerses itself in nature the more the human being feels when it has to change and how much it has to preserve in its own life and its relations.

Indigenous peoples are the best example for us of how to listen to nature. Because of their profound affinity with nature, with the land, the rains, the clouds, the winds, the waters, the plants and the animals, they know at once what is going to happen and what they have to do. They are so united with the Earth as Earth's sons and daughters, they are so united with the Earth as the talking and thinking Earth itself, that they immediately catch what is going to happen in nature. That is, nature speaks to them and through them.

Investigations carried out in great metropolitan European and North American centres established that a greater knowledge of the ecological crises and of the wounds of the Earth does not necessarily lead to a transformation of attitudes towards more respect and veneration for the Earth. These investigations assert that the most important thing is not to know, but to feel. The more a person suffers with the degradation of the environment, the more that person becomes indignant at the sufferings of animals and revolts against the destruction of the green land of the Earth, the more that person will develop new attitudes of compassion, of tenderness, of protection towards nature, and a cosmic spirituality.

Once more we encounter pathos, the profound feeling at the root of the new paradigm of living together with the Earth. From listening to the Earth and from passion for her emerges essential care. Without careful listening we cannot hear the great voice of the Earth calling us to enter into synergy, to feel compassion, and to create a peaceful co-existence with all beings.

This attitude is required, for instance, within the scope of biotechnology, one of the most advanced fields of science. What is the right measure of intervention in the human genetic code? This is not written anywhere. The human being needs to establish this starting point from a profound sensitivity and communion with life itself. If the human being enters the laboratory of genetic experimentation as someone who enters a temple and conducts the processes as someone who performs a liturgy – since life is mysterious and sacred and demands attitudes of reverence – the human being will feel, more than simply knowing, what can and cannot be done. This is feeling loaded with care, responsibility and compassion. Starting from this pathos it becomes absurd to desire to subordinate the new knowledge in genetics for the making of profit, as if life were a simple commodity put on a counter to be bought and sold.

The attitude of feeling with care must become a culture, and this demands a pedagogical process that goes beyond formal schooling, that transcends institutions and that gives rise to a new state of conscience and of connection with the Earth and with everything that exists and lives in the Earth.

As is so well stated in Psalm 119.19 we will feel 'sojourners' on the Earth; we are respectful guests of the innkeeper Earth. And as such we leave the common home always tidy for the other guests that will come after us.

Vital tenderness

Vital tenderness is synonymous with essential care. Tenderness is the affection that we devote to people and the care that we apply to existential situations. It is a knowledge that goes beyond reason since it shows itself as an intelligence that is intuitive, that sees further and that establishes communion. Tenderness is care without obsession: it also encompasses work, not as a mere utilitarian form of production, but as a workmanship that expresses the creativity and self-fulfilment of people. Tenderness is not effeminacy nor it is the rejection of rigour in knowledge. It is a feeling of affection that, in its own way, also knows. In fact we only know something well when we nourish it with affection and when we feel ourselves involved with that which we wish to know. Tenderness can and must go side by side with extreme commitment to a cause, as was exemplarily demonstrated by the great revolutionary Che Guevara (1928–67). From him we inherit the inspiring phrase: '*Hay que endurecer pero sin perder la ternura jamás*' (One has to grow hard but without ever losing tenderness).

Tenderness emerges from the very act of existing in the world with others. We do not exist, we co-exist, we co-live and we commune with those realities that are close to us. We feel our fundamental connection with the totality of the world. This feeling is more than a psychological motion; it is an existential way of being that is intertwined through all beings. But if we focus on sentiment it generates sentimentalism, which is the product of a subjectivity that is badly integrated. It is the subject that unfolds upon itself and celebrates its own sensations. Tenderness, on the contrary, emerges when the subject decentralizes itself from itself, goes in the direction of the other, feels the other as another, participates in the other's existence and lets itself be touched by the other's life history. The other marks the subject. The subject focuses on the other not because of the sensations that the other causes upon itself, but because of love, because of esteem for the other's difference and because of the value of the other's life and strivings.

The relation of tenderness does not involve anguish because it is free from the search for advantage and domination. The feeling of tenderness is the proper power of the heart; it is the deep desire to share journeys. The other's anguish is my anguish, the other's success is my success, and the other's salvation or perdition is my salvation or perdition; it is not just mine but of all human beings.

Blaise Pascal, French philosopher and mathematician of the seventeenth century, introduced an important distinction that helps us to understand care and tenderness: *esprit de finesse* and *esprit de géometrie*.

The *esprit de finesse* is the spirit of finesse, of sensitivity, of care and of tenderness. Spirit does not only think and feel. It goes beyond this by adding on sensitivity, intuition and the capacity to unify itself with rationality and with thinking. From the spirit of finesse emerges the world of excellence, of great meanings, of values and commitments on which it is worth spending energy and time.

The *esprit de géométrie* is the spirit of calculations and workmanship, which is interested in efficiency and power. It is the way-of-being that has reigned in modern days. It has put aside, under much suspicion, everything that has to do with affection, with tenderness and with essential care. From this fact also derives the terrifying emptiness of our 'geometric' culture with its plethora of sensations but without deep experiential meaning; with its fantastic accumulation of knowledge but with scant wisdom; with too much emphasis on muscle power, sexuality, artefacts of destruction which are shown in serial-killer films, a culture without tenderness and care towards the Earth, towards the sons and daughters of the Earth, towards the common future of all.

Essential caress

Caress constitutes one of the greatest expressions of care. Why do I say 'essential caress'? Because I want to set it apart from caress as pure psychological excitement caused by a demonstration of affection that is short-lived and without a history. Caress excitement does not encompass the whole of the person. Caress is essential when it transforms itself in an attitude, in a way of being that qualifies the person in its totality, in its psyche, its thinking, its will, its subjectivity and in the relations it establishes.

The organ of caress is, fundamentally, the hand: the hand that touches, the hand that strokes, the hand that establishes relations, the hand that lulls, the hand that brings calm. But the hand is not simply a hand. It is the person that through the hand and in the hand reveals a caring way-of-being. Caress touches the innermost recesses of the human being, there where its personal centre is situated. In order for caress to be truly essential it needs to touch the inner I and not only the superficial ego of consciousness.

Caress that emerges from the centre confers tranquillity, integration and assurance, and thus the meaning of caressing. When the mother caresses the child, the mother communicates to the child the most orientating experience that exists: the fundamental assurance of the goodness of reality and of the universe; the assurance that in the end everything has a meaning; the assurance that peace and not conflict is the ultimate word; the assurance of welcoming and not of exclusion from the great Womb.

As with tenderness, caress demands total altruism, respect for the other and renunciation of any intention other than that of experiencing affection and love. It is not a rubbing of skins but an investment of affection and of love through the hand and through the skin.

Affection does not exist without caress, tenderness and care. Just as the star needs its aura to shine, affection needs caress to survive. It is the caressing of the skin, hair, hands, face, shoulders and in sexual intimacy that confers concreteness to affection and to love. It is the quality of caress that prevents affection from being a liar, false or dubious. Essential caress is as subtle as the careful, partial opening of a door. There is never caress in the violent breaking down of doors and windows, that is to say, in the invasion of the intimacy of a person.

The Colombian psychiatrist Luis Carlos Restrepo said with accuracy: 'The hand, a human organ par excellence, can be used either to caress or to seize. The hand that seizes and the hand that caresses are two extreme facets of the possibilities in inter-human encounter.'[2] Within the context of my reflections the hand that seizes personifies the way-of-being through work. To seize is an expression of power over, manipulation of, and of the fitting of the other, or of things, into one's own way of being. The hand that caresses represents the way-of-being through care since 'caress is a hand covered in patience that touches without wounding and that is free so that it allows the mobility of the being with whom we enter into contact.'[3]

Fundamental cordiality

The right measure, vital tenderness, essential caress and fundamental cordiality are existential qualities; that is to say, they are forms of structuring the human being in that which makes it a human being. Care, with its resonances, is the artisan of our humanity. This is also true for cordiality, which has been so badly interpreted in Brazilian culture since it was introduced as a category of sociological analysis at the end of the 1930s.

Normally, cordiality is taken as an expression of emotion in its psychological sense, in contrast to rationality. It is said that Brazilians are cordial: in fact the Brazilian is. Brazilians put more heart than logic into things. But be careful! The heart-emotivity can produce as much politeness, sense of hospitality and exuberance contained in pleasure, as it can produce outbursts of violence and deep hatred, which are typical of certain families in the sugar-cane plantation areas of the Brazilian northeast. These contradictions are more apparent in the national elites than in the popular strata since historically the national elites 'castrated and re-castrated, bled and re-bled the Brazilian people'.[4]

When I speak of cordiality as a resonance of care I think of it in a different way. I see the heart as a dimension of the *esprit de finesse*, as the capacity to catch the dimension of value that is present in people and in things. The important things are not the facts per se, but that which the facts produce that is meaningful for us, and as such enriches and transforms us. Here emerges the dimension of value, of that which counts, has weight and definitely interests us. Value transforms facts into symbols and into sacraments. They are no longer facts that have happened and that have passed; they become bearers of evocation, meaning and memory.

Now, it is the particular role of the heart to catch the axiomatic and value-based dimension of the Being in its totality and in its manifestations in concrete entities. Thus, cordiality means that way of being that discovers a beating heart in everything, in every stone, in every star and in every person. It is that attitude that is so well portrayed by the Little Prince: 'It is only with the heart that one sees rightly.'[5] The heart is able to see beyond the facts; it sees the union with the whole; it discerns meanings and discovers values. Cordiality presupposes the capacity to feel the other's heart and the hidden heart of all things. The cordial person listens, puts its ear close to reality, pays attention and puts care in all things.

In Latin America it was the Náhuatl culture of the Aztecs of Mexico that ascribed special significance to the heart. Their definition of a human being was not, as among us, the definition of a rational animal; it was rather the definition of 'an owner of a face and of a heart'. The face identifies and differentiates a human being from other human beings. Through the face the human being establishes an ethical intercourse with the other. Our faces show if we welcome the other, if we distrust the other, if we exclude the other. The heart, in turn, defines the way-of-being and the character of the person; it is the vital principle from where all actions spring.

The refined education of the Aztecs, which was preserved in wonderful texts, aimed to establish among the young a face that was clear, good and without shadows, along with a heart that was firm and warm, determined and welcoming, sympathetic and respectful of the sacred things. According to the Aztecs it was through the heart that emerged the religion that used 'the flower and the song' to venerate its deities. They put their heart into everything that they did. This cor-diality[6] showed in the works of art that they created. The great German painter from the Renaissance period, Albrecht Dürer, after contemplating in 1520 Aztec objects of art which had been given to the Emperor Charles V by Hernan Cortés, registered in his diary the following account: 'In my whole life I have not seen anything that has brought as much joy to my heart as these things. In them I have found objects that are wonderfully artistic and I am amazed by the subtle geniality of the people of these strange lands.'[7] This was the resonance of care and compassion expressing itself in the Aztecs' objects of art.

Necessary living together

Along with cordiality comes living together. Living together as a concept was put forward by Ivan Illich, one of the great Latin American prophets. He was born in Vienna in 1926 and worked in Latin America and with Latinos in the USA. Through the concept of living together he tried to give the answer to two current crises, which are intimately interlinked: the crisis of the industrial process and the ecological crisis.

Let us first look at the crisis of the industrial process. The relation of the human being to the instrument has become the relation of the instrument to the human being. Created to substitute the slave, the technological instrument ended up enslaving the human being who aimed for mass production. It gave rise to a society of apparatus, but without soul. The industrial production currently in place does not combine with the imagination and creativity of the workers. From these it only wants to use their work strength, muscular or intellectual. When it stimulates creativity the aim is the quality of the product as a whole, which is of more benefit to the company than to the worker.

That said, however, it is a sign of our times that many businessmen and businesswomen have become aware of this distortion and have directly confronted the dehumanization of industrial society. Many have placed on the company's agenda a discussion of the new paradigm of re-connection, subjectivity, spirituality and relations of cooperation and synergy between all, businesspeople and workers.

What do I understand of living together? I understand the capacity to make the dimensions of production and care, of affection and compassion, live together; the careful moulding of everything that we produce using creativity, freedom and imagination; the ability to maintain the multidimensional balance between society and nature, and the reassuring feeling of mutual belonging.

Living together aims to combine the technical value of material production with the ethical value of social and spiritual production. After having elaborated the economy of material goods it is important urgently to develop the economy of human qualities. Is not the greatest resource, infinite and inexhaustible, perchance the human being?

The human values of sensitivity, care, living together and veneration can impose limits upon the voracity of power-domination and production-exploration.

In the second place, living together is the ultimate answer to the ecological crises caused by the industrial process of the past four centuries: a process that lacks a sense of responsibility for depredations on the environment and that can cause dramatic devastation to the Earth-system and to all of its regulating organizations.

This scenario is not far-fetched. It happened before, when Wall Street crashed in 1929. On that occasion it was only a partial crisis of the capitalist system. Now it is about a crisis of the global system. Within a context of generalized disruption the first reaction of the ruling system will certainly be to increase its global control and to use massive force to safeguard the maintenance of the productive process and of the financial system. Such diligence, instead of alleviating the crisis, will deepen it because of the growth in technological unemployment and the inefficacy of policies for the integration of victims within one global society.

According to Illich the crisis may transform itself into a catastrophe of apocalyptic dimensions. But it may also be the only chance to define the caring use of technological instruments in the service of the preservation of the planet, for the welfare of humanity, and to cooperation between peoples.

To reach this new level, humanity will probably have to experience a sinister Good Friday which will hurl into the abyss the dictatorship of the way-of-being through work-material-production. Only then can it be Resurrection Sunday, the reconstruction of the global society based on care.

The first paragraph of the new social pact between the surviving peoples will establish the sacred decision of self-limitation and of duty to live by the right measure, having care towards the inheritance that we have received from the universe, having essential tenderness towards human beings and having respect towards the other beings of creation. Production will be intimately linked to the idea of living together since it will guarantee enough to attend to human necessities and be appropriate to carry out projects that show solidarity. The human being will learn to use technological instruments as means and not as ends; and we will learn to live together with all things as brothers and sisters and will know how to treat all things with reverence and respect.

When this very fortunate event occurs, the new millennium will be inaugurated with the establishing of a new paradigm of civilization that is more favourable to life, with justice and affection between all.

Radical compassion

The last aspect of care, radical compassion, represents the major contribution of Buddhism to humanity. Radical compassion is considered to be the personal virtue of the Buddha, whose real name is Siddhartha Gautama, who lived during the sixth and fifth centuries BCE. Compassion is part of the basic experience of Buddhism, and it articulates two different, but complementary, movements: total detachment from the world through asceticism, and care for the world through compassion. Through detachment the human being liberates itself from the enslaving desire for possession and accumulation. Through care the human being re-connects itself to the world in an affectionate way, taking responsibility for it.

Com-passion[8] is not a minor feeling of 'pity' towards those who suffer. It is not passive but extremely active. Com-passion, as the Latin philology of the word suggests, is the capacity to share passion with the other. It is about coming out of one's own sphere and entering into the universe of the other to suffer with the other, to be happy with the other, to walk with the other and to build life in synergy with the other.

In the first instance this attitude brings about the renouncing of domination and ultimately of killing any living being, and the refusal to commit any form of violence against nature. In the second instance this attitude seeks to build communion, starting from those who are suffering more and who are more penalized. It is only by starting from these last ones that the door to a society that is really integrating and inclusive is opened. The Chinese philosophy of feng shui, as we shall see, proposes a careful way of treating nature and of ecologically organizing gardens and human homes.

In Hinduism we find the concept of *ahimsa* which corresponds to Buddhist com-passion. It is the attitude of non-violence through which one seeks to avoid causing any sort of suffering or constraint to other beings. Many Hindu holy texts teach treating all beings with the same care and with the same reverence that one treats children. Gandhi was the modern genius of *ahimsa*.

The Tao tradition knows a similar concept, *wu wei*. It is an active virtue: harmonizing with the measure of each thing, leaving it be and not interfering. When one renounces things, fighting against one's will to possess, one exercises *wu wei*; that is to say, one enters into communion with things, one catches their dance as well as dancing together with them.

The Judaeo-Christian tradition knows *rachamim* or mercy. In Hebrew *rachamim* means to have entrails and to feel with them the reality of the other, especially of those who suffer. It means therefore to feel with, rather than to understand, and to show the capacity to identify and to feel compassion for the other. Mercy is considered the basic characteristic of the spiritual experience of Jesus of Nazareth. He experienced and announced a Father God whose mercy does not have limits: 'gives sun and rain to the just and the unjust' (Matthew 5.45) and does not stop 'loving the ungrateful and the wicked' (Luke 6.35).[9] It is the merciful God with a prodigal son, with the strayed sheep, and with the public sinner. It is a Father with characteristics of Mother. And Jesus himself shows mercy towards those who have taken him to the cross.

Psalm 103 expresses very well the divine focus on mercy:

> The LORD is merciful and gracious, slow to anger and abounding in steadfast love . . . As a father pities his children, so the LORD pities those who fear him. For he knows our frame; he remembers that we are dust . . . But the steadfast love of the LORD is from everlasting to everlasting.   (Psalm 103.8–17)

In the supreme moment, when everything is decided, we will be judged by the minimum of the com-passion and of the mercy that we showed towards those who have hunger, are thirsty, are without clothes or imprisoned (cf. Matthew 25.36–46).[10] The criterion for com-passion is identical for Christians, Egyptians and Tibetans, and it is widely commented on in their respective sacred books.

In conclusion, these resonances, among others, are echoes of essential care. They are different voices singing the same lullaby. It is love, right measure, tenderness, caress, cordiality, living together and compassion that guarantee the humanity of human beings. Through these ways-of-being, human beings continuously fulfil their autopoiesis; that is to say, their historical self-fulfilment, simultaneously building the Earth and preserving the tribes of the Earth with their cultures, their values, their dreams and their spiritual traditions.

9

Concretizations of care

After having characterized the way-of-being through care, it is important now to demonstrate the ways through which it becomes concrete. I shall start with more general examples and then arrive at more particular ones.

Care for our unique planet

Our planet Earth deserves very special care. We only have this planet on which to live and have our being. It is a system of systems and a supraorganism of complex equilibrium that was woven over millions and millions of years. Because of the predatory assault of the industrial process that occurred in the past centuries this balance is about to be broken by a chain reaction. Since the beginning of industrialization, in the eighteenth century, the global population has grown eight times, increasingly consuming more natural resources; and production based on the exploitation of nature has grown more than 100 times. The aggravation of this scenario and the globalization of productive processes increase the threat to, and consequently the necessity of essential care for, the future of the Earth.

The collective consciousness concerned with our beautiful planet is small. Those who could bring awareness about this issue to humanity instead enjoy their voyage in the *Titanic* of illusions. They hardly realize that we may be about to encounter an ecological iceberg that will cause us to sink very quickly.

The fact that there is a lack of investment in the global management of the problems of the Earth is tragic. The UN manages about 40 projects that are concerned with global problems, such as climate, deforestation, pollution of the air, soil and water, famine, spread of epidemics, problems impinging on the young and the elderly, migration, and others. The UN is dominated by the old paradigm of imperialist nations who see the nation state and the power blocs, but who have yet to discover the Earth as an object that requires care, that requires a collective policy of terrestrial salvation.

In order to care for the planet we all need to pass through a process of learning the ecological ABC and reviewing our habits of consumption. It is important to develop an ethic of care.

The United Nations Environment Programme (UNEP), the World Wide Fund for Nature (WWF) and the World Conservation Union (IUCN), elaborated a very detailed strategy for the future of life under the title *Caring for the Earth* in 1991.[1] Here they established nine principles for the sustainability* of the Earth. They projected a global strategy founded on care:

1 building a sustainable society
2 respecting and caring for the community of life
3 improving the quality of human life
4 conserving the Earth's vitality and diversity
5 keeping within the Earth's carrying capacity
6 changing personal attitudes and practices
7 enabling communities to care for their own environments
8 providing a national framework for integrating development and conservation
9 creating a global alliance.

These principles embody essential care for the Earth. Essential care is the ethic of a sustainable planet. It is rightly stated in *Caring for the Earth* that: 'The ethic of care applies at the international as well as the national and individual levels. All nations stand to gain from worldwide sustainability – and are threatened if we fail to attain it.'² Only this ethic of essential care can save us from the worst. Only this ethic can open for us a horizon of future and of hope.

Care for the environment itself

Care for the Earth represents the global. Care for the environment itself represents the local. The human being has its feet on the ground (local) and its head open to the infinite (global). The heart unites the ground to the infinite, abyss and stars, local and global. The logic of the heart is the capacity to find the right measure and to implement the dynamic balance.

For this reason each person needs to discover him- or herself as part of the local ecosystem and of the biotic community, with reference to both its natural aspect and its cultural dimension. One needs to get to know one's brothers and sisters who share the same atmosphere, the same scenery, the same soil, the same springs, the same nourishing sources; one needs to know the kind of plants, animals and microorganisms that inhabit the common environmental niche; one needs to know the history of the scenery, to visit its rivers and mountains, to frequent its waterfalls and caves; one needs to know the history of the peoples who lived there, their saga and who built their habitat, the way they worked with nature, the way they preserved or wrecked nature, who were their poets and sages, heroes and heroines, saints, founding fathers and/or mothers of their local civilization.

All this means taking care of the environmental locality itself, living in it from the heart as one's own extended body, discovering the reasons to preserve it and to help it develop within the dynamics of the native ecosystem.

What is good for the individual is good for the local community. The local community also needs to tread the pathway of entering into the local ecosystem and of looking after the environment; it needs to use resources in a frugal fashion, minimizing the erosion of those resources, recycling materials and preserving biodiversity. It must get to know its history, its main characters and its folklore. It must take care of its city, its squares and public places, its dwellings and schools, its hospitals and places of worship, its theatres, its cinemas, its sports stadiums, its monuments, and the collective memory of its people. Hence, for instance, it chooses to plant in parks and public streets plant species of the local ecosystem, and it prefers local and regional cuisine in restaurants.

This care for the ecological locality will only become real if there is a collective process of education, in which the majority takes part, has access to information and engages in an exchange of knowledge. That is, to take popular knowledge that is contained in the traditions of the elderly, in the legends and in the stories of the indigenous Indians, caboclos, blacks, mestizos, immigrants, of those who first lived in the area, and confront and complement it with critical and scientific knowledge.[3] This knowledge reveals dimensions of the local reality and is loaded with truth and deep meaning that is to be deciphered and taken in by all. The result of this is a profound and dynamic harmony of the ecosystem where living and inert entities, cultural and social institutions, at last all find their place, interact with each other, welcome each other, complement each other and feel themselves at home.

Care for the sustainable society

Currently almost all societies are sick. They generate a bad quality of life for all – human beings and the other beings of the natural world. And this could not be different since the foundations of these societies rest on the way-of-being through work, which is understood as the domination and exploitation of nature and of the work of the labourer. There are exceptions to these societies, such as the societies of indigenous Indians and of other minorities of Southeast Asia,

Oceania and the Arctic region, but all of these are hostage to a kind of development that attends to the necessities of only a part of humankind (i.e. industrialized countries), who leave the remaining part of humankind in need, and in some cases leads straight into famine and dire poverty. We are a species that has shown itself capable of oppressing and massacring its own brothers and sisters in a very cruel and merciless fashion. In the twentieth century about 200 million people died in wars, massacres and concentration camps. And even today societies based on the way-of-being through work degenerate and destroy their foundations of non-renewable natural resources.

It is not about putting *Limits to Growth* (which is the title of the first report presented in 1972 to the Club of Rome) but a change in the kind of development.[4] It is said that new development must be sustainable. Development per se does not exist; what really occurs is that a society opts for the kind of development it wants and requires. When one speaks of a sustainable society or of a sustainable planet, one should understand these as necessary preconditions for a truly encompassing form of development.

What is sustainable is the society or the planet that produces sufficient for itself and for the beings in the ecosystem in which it is situated; that takes from nature only that which nature can replace; that shows a sense of solidarity between generations since it preserves for the societies of the future the resources they will need. In practice, society must show itself capable of taking on new habits and planning a type of development that cultivates care for the ecological balance and that functions within the limits imposed by nature. This does not mean a return to the past; it rather means to offer a new focus for the common future. It is not simply about not consuming, but about consuming responsibly.

The moving force behind this kind of development is neither located in the market, nor in the state, nor in the public sector, nor in the production of wealth. Rather, it is located in the human person, in the community and in the remaining beings who share with the human being the terrestrial adventure.

Development is here conceived within another paradigm that has been taken on by certain sectors of the UN. In the well-known 'Declaration on the Rights to Development' of 4 December 1986, the High Commission for Human Rights of the UN declared:

> development is a comprehensive economic, social, cultural and political process, which aims at the constant improvement of the well-being of the entire population and of all individuals on the basis of their active, free and meaningful participation in development and in the fair distribution of benefits resulting therefrom.[5]

I would add here also, to be more integrating, the psychological and spiritual dimensions of the human being.

To state this in simple terms, social development aims at improving the quality of human life qua human. In universal values this implies a healthy and long life, education, political participation, democracy that is social and participative and not merely representative, guaranteed respect for human rights and protection against violence, and conditions for appropriate expression of symbolic and spiritual values. All these values are reached only if there is care in the collective effort of building society, if there is a sense of living together between those who are different, cordiality in social interaction, compassion towards all those who suffer and who feel marginalized, and with the creation of strategies of compensation and integration. The sick, the elderly, the carriers of some sort of social stigma, the marginalized and excluded deserve special care. Through them is measured how much sustainability and how much essential care has been and is being realized in society. Beyond all this, it is important to cultivate understanding, remarkable patience, capacity for dialogue and a sense of creative integration with reference to the diabolical and demented side of human history. All these values are integral to essential care.

Care for the other, animus and anima

There is not just a web of social relations. There are concrete people, men and women. As human beings, people are speaking entities, and through speech they build the world with their interactions. For this reason, the human being is, in essence, someone with unlimited relations. The I only emerges through the dialogue with the Thou, as has been recognized by modern psychologists, and before them by philosophers of the personalism movement.[6] The Thou comes before the I. The Thou is the midwife of the I.

The Thou, however, is not an undefined thing. It is a real face that looks and that has an expression. The face of the other makes indifference impossible, the face of the other forces me to take a position because it speaks, pro-vokes, e-vokes, and con-vokes.[7] and especially the face of the impoverished, the marginalized, and the excluded.

The face possesses a way of looking and an aura that no one can take away. The face and the way of looking always launch a pro-posal in search of a res-ponse. It is through this that res-ponsi-bility arises, the obligation to give res-ponses. Here we find the birthplace of the ethic that focuses on the relation of res-ponsi-bility[8] when faced by the face of the other, especially by the face of the other who is oppressed. It is in the embracing or in the rejection, in the alliance with or in the hostility towards the face of the other that the most primary relations of human beings are established and where the tendency for domination or cooperation is decided.

Care for the other involves keeping an observant eye on this dialogue, this dialogical action I–Thou, so that it is libertarian, synergetic and able to build an enduring alliance of peace and love.

The 'other' always occurs in the form of a man or a woman. These are different but they meet on the same common ground that is humanity. Both fulfil, in their own particular way, the human essence that is unfathomable and mysterious. The difference between them is not something closed and defined but something always open and shapeable since they always find themselves in constant interaction and reciprocity.

In the language coined by C. G. Jung, each one possesses within him- or herself the animus; that is, the masculine dimension, and the anima; that is, the feminine dimension. The man awakes in the woman her masculine dimension culturally expressed in the way-of-being through work, and the woman evokes in the man his feminine dimension which is historically concretized by the way-of-being through care.

Care for the other's animus-anima implies an enormous effort to overcome gender domination, to dismantle patriarchalism and chauvinism on the one hand, and matriarchalism and exclusive feminism on the other. It requires us to conceive relations that favour the manifestation of differences in such a way that these are no longer understood as inequalities but as the unique and complex richness of human substance. This convergence in diversity creates the space for a more global and integrated experience of our own humanity, a more caring way of being.

Care for the poor, the oppressed and the excluded

One of the major challenges faced by ethically guided politics and by the way-of-being through care is undoubtedly the millions and millions of poor, oppressed and excluded in our societies. This widespread situation results from the highly unjust ways of organizing society which are currently in force globally. Indeed, thanks to technological advances in the past

decades we have experienced a fantastic growth in the generation of services and the production of material goods, which,
however, have been distributed in a callous way by forcing two-
thirds of humanity to live in dire poverty. Nothing is more
damaging to the way-of-being through care than cruelty
towards our own equals.

How are we to deal with the condemned and offended of
the Earth? The answer to this question divides, from top to
bottom, public policies, humanistic traditions, religions and
the Christian churches. Increasingly the conviction grows that
strategies solely based on aid, and that are paternalistic, do not
solve, as they never have done, the problems of the poor and
excluded. Rather, these strategies perpetuate the problem since
they maintain the poor and excluded in a condition of depend-
ence and of begging, humiliating them by not recognizing their
strength to transform society.

The liberation of the oppressed will come from themselves.
As they become conscious of the injustice of their situation they
organize themselves and start to implement practices that aim
to structurally transform unequal social relations. Siding with
the poor in their fight against poverty and in favour of their
life and freedom was and still is the registered trademark of community groups and churches that started to listen to the cry of
the poor, who can be exploited workers, indigenous Indians,
blacks who suffer discrimination, or oppressed women and
marginalized minorities, or those who are carriers of the Aids
virus (those who are HIV positive) or of any other affliction.
Those who are not oppressed but who have allied themselves
with the oppressed are not a few. They, together with and from
the perspective of the oppressed, strive to bring about profound
social changes.

The commitment of the oppressed and their allies to a
new kind of society, in which the exploitation of the human
being and the plundering of the Earth is overcome, reveals the
political strength of the dimension of care.

What is the ultimate moving force underlying the organized movement of the landless, of the homeless, of those who are deprived of social rights, of the street children, of the elderly, of the peoples of the jungle, to name a few – what else but care for human life? It is care and the feeling of being touched by the inalienable dignity of life that moves people and movements to protest, to resist and to mobilize themselves to change history. The ancient and modern prophets show us the co-existence of these two attitudes that are present in political care: the firm denunciation of oppressors and the feeling of being touched through the consolation of their victims.

If one does not care for those who are impoverished and excluded one does not truly love them and does not take any risks for their cause. The consolidation of the globalized world society and the rise of a new paradigm of civilization occurs through care for the poor, marginalized and excluded. If their problems are not resolved, we will remain within pre-historic times. We may have started a new millennium, but we have not established a new civilization and an era of eternal peace between all humans, all created beings and our splendid planet.

Care for our body in sickness and in health

When we speak about the body we should not think about it in the usual sense of the word, which contrasts the body to the soul, matter to spirit. In this sense, body is a part of the human being and not a human being's totality. Modern sciences prefer to speak of corporeity* to express the human being as a live and organic whole. And there is also talk of the human being-body and the human being-soul to designate particular dimensions of the human being.

Such an understanding of the human being leaves behind the dualism of body and soul and establishes a more encompassing view of the human being. Between matter and spirit is life, which is the interaction of matter that becomes increasingly more complex, that interiorizes itself and that organizes itself. The body is always enlivened. As a spiritual sage once said: 'To care for someone's body is to be concerned with the breath that livens up him or her.'

In short, it can be said that the body is that part of the universe that we enliven, that we inquire about, that we give conscience to, that we personalize. The body is made of cosmic dust that has been circulating in interstellar space for billions of years, that was circulating even before the formation of galaxies, stars and planets, cosmic dust which is certainly older than our solar system and the Earth itself. The iron that runs through the veins of the body, the phosphorus and the calcium that strengthen the bones and nerves, the 18 per cent of carbon and the 65 per cent of oxygen demonstrate that we are truly cosmic entities.

The body is a live ecosystem that is linked to other more encompassing systems. We belong to the *Homo* species that belongs to the system Earth that belongs to the galactic system and to the cosmic system. Within the body there functions an internal system that regulates cold and heat, sleep and wakefulness, that regulates the phenomena of digestion, breathing, the heartbeat, and others.

Moreover, the live body is subjectivity. It has already been said that 'the body is our most archaic memory' because in its wholeness and in each of its parts it keeps information of the long evolutionary process. Throughout the lifespan of the body various levels of consciousness are realized (i.e. the ordinary, the oral, the anal, the social, the autonomous and the transcendental), where these memories are expressed and enriched through interaction with the environment.

Through the body the fragility of the human being is shown. Corporeal life is mortal. It loses its energetic assets, its balance, it becomes ill and finally dies. Death does not come at the end of life. It rather starts with the first moment of life.

We start dying, slowly, until the moment when we finally finish dying. Acceptance of the mortality of life allows us to understand sickness and health in a different light.

A healthy person can become sick. Sickness means damage to the totality of existence. It is not my knee that hurts. It is I, in my totality of existence, who suffer. Therefore, it is not a part that is sick; it is rather life that becomes ill in its various dimensions. That is, in relation to itself (i.e. it experiences the limits of mortal life), in relation to society (i.e. it isolates itself, it stops working and it must be treated in a health centre), in relation to the global meaning of life (i.e. an upset of the fundamental trust in life, which makes life ask itself: Why did I become sick?).

Sickness is connected to health. Any cure must reintegrate the dimensions of a healthy life at its personal and social levels as well as at its fundamental level, which is connected to the absolute meaning of existence and of the universe. For this reason the first step consists in strengthening the health dimension so that it can cure the sickness dimension.

To strengthen the health dimension we must enrich our understanding of health. We should not understand health as the dominating practice with its sophisticated techniques and innumerable cocktails of vitamins. Within this perspective, health is conceived as 'total health', as if it was an end in itself, and it does not address the fundamental question: What do I do in life with my health? We have distanced ourselves from the World Health Organization's definition of health (the United Nations specialized agency for health), which is: 'a state of complete physical, mental, spiritual and social well being and not merely the absence of disease or infirmity'.[9]

The current dominant understanding is not realistic because it starts from the false premise that an existence without pain and death is possible. It is also non-human because it does not acknowledge the reality of life, which is mortality. It does not discover within itself death and its companions, its ailments, weaknesses, infirmities, agonies and the final farewell. Furthermore, health is not such a state as the dominant understanding holds, but a permanent process of seeking the dynamic equilibrium of the various factors that constitute life. All these factors are at the service of the person so that it has the power to be autonomous, free, open and creative in the face of the various challenges that it confronts.

The power to be a person means the capacity to welcome life as it is in itself, with its realities and its intrinsic jubilation, but also with its finitude and its mortality. The power to be a person translates into the capacity to live together, to grow with and to humanize these dimensions of life, sickness and death.

Health and healing designate a process of adaptation and of integration with the most diverse situations, where health, sickness, suffering, recovering, ageing and the peaceful progress towards the great passage to death occur. Therefore, health is neither a state nor an existential act; it is rather an attitude in the face of the various situations which can be either of sickness or health. To be a person is not simply to be healthy but to know how to face sickness and health in a healthy way. To be healthy means to realize a meaning of life that encompasses health, sickness and death. Someone can be deadly sick and at the same time be healthy because with this deadly situation this person grows, humanizes him- or herself, and knows how to give meaning to that which endures suffering.

As a respectful German doctor once said: 'Health is not the absence of sickness. Health is the strength to live with sickness.' Health is to welcome and to love life as life presents itself, happy and laborious, healthy and ailing, limited and open to the unlimited that will come after death.

Thus, according to this understanding, what does it mean to care for our body? It is a huge task. It implies to care for the life that enlivens it, to care for the various relations between the body and the reality that surrounds it, relations which have bearings on hygiene, on eating habits, on the air that is breathed, on the way we dress, on the way in which we organize our home and in which we situate ourselves in a given ecological space. Care for all these things reinforces our identity as beings-of-relation in all directions. To care for the body means to search for the creative assimilation of everything that can occur in life, commitments and tasks, meaningful encounters and existential crises, successes and failures, health and suffering. Only as such can we increasingly become mature, autonomous, wise and utterly free people.

Care for the integral cure of the human being

The integral cure of the human being is so important that it demands that I take the above reflections further. In the great therapeutic traditions of humanity there has always been the understanding that cure is a global process that involves the totality of the human being and not only the part of the human being that is ill. It is worth mentioning here two figures of the Western tradition, Asclepius (of the Greeks) and Aesculapius (of the Romans), and from this tradition comes the father of classic and modern medicine, Hippocrates (460–377 BCE).

Asclepius was, historically, a healing hero whose main centre was in Epidaurus, in the heart of Greece. For more than a thousand years the sick from all corners of the ancient world rushed to his temple. The efficacy of his methods was such that after his death Asclepius ended up being divinized. As both man and god Asclepius indicated that a cure is only complete if it is the result of human and divine intervention, if it is corporal and spiritual.

In the portico of Asclepius' temple the sick could read the fundamental motto of his medicine: 'Pure must be he who enters the fragrant temple; purity means to think nothing but holy thoughts.'[10]

This was called *noostherapy*, the therapy of the mind (*noos* or *nous* in Greek means a process of redefinition of attitudes and values).[11] To this day Christians call this process 'conversion' (*metanoia*). Sins (*hamatia*) – that is, those disharmonious attitudes within oneself, with others, with the cosmos, and with the original Fountain of all – trigger processes that affect the physico-chemical-spiritual equilibrium of the human being. In other words, the processes that generate diseases.

Cure happens when a new balance is established in the human being. As such, the disease of sin gives way to the cure of grace. In Epidaurus cures were organized in a holistic fashion and through the use of different methods: dance, music, gymnastics, poetry, rites and sacred sleep. There was the *abaton*, a sanctuary where the sick slept in order to have dreams of communion with the deity who would touch and heal them. There was the *odeon*, a place where one could listen to calming music and where elevating poems were read. There was the *gymnasium*, where physical exercises that aimed at the integration of mind and body were practised. There was the *stadium* for controlled competitive sports that aimed to improve the vigour of the body. There was the *theatron* for the dramatization of complex situations of life so that these situations were dedramatized and thus facilitated cure. There was the *bibliotheke* where one could consult books, admire works of art and take part in discussions about the most diverse topics. All these were already seen in those days as forms of holistic therapy. Modern alternative medicine does nothing new; it is merely recovering this therapeutic memory of our own tradition, which was suppressed by the dominating scientific paradigm that tries to cure by focusing on the treatment of the parts that are ill through the use of the chemistry of medicines, without taking into account the whole of the human being.

It was within this integrating context of total care for the human being that the poet Juvenal, Decimus Junius Juvenalis

(60–130 CE) wrote the famous verse criticizing the excesses of Roman gastronomy: '*Orandum est ut sit mens sana in corpore sano*', 'You should pray for a healthy mind in a healthy body' (*Satires x*, 356).

Many modern sports centres have taken the motto, *mens sana in corpore sano*, almost always forgetting the spiritual dimension of the mind (*mens sana*) and emphasizing the muscular exuberance of the body (*corpore sano*). The art of therapy is more than merely medicinal; it is integral, and therefore it is deeply spiritual.

To conclude, to care for our health means to maintain an integral perspective, always searching to build a balance between the body, the mind and the spirit, and to summon the doctor (body), the therapist (mind), and the priest (spirit) to work together with the totality of the human being in mind.

Care for our soul: interior angels and demons

The soul, in a similar way as it happens with the body, is a representation of the totality of the human being in so far as the human being is a live being with interiority and subjectivity (*anima* in Latin means a live being, and from this we get our word 'animal'). From the first moment after the big bang, when the first energetic fields were formed and when the first relations were forged, the soul started to emerge and to get more complex to the point where, at the level of the human being and after the appearance of the brain and of the neural network, it became capable of reflection and self-consciousness. This possibly occurred first with *Homo Ardipithecus Ramidus* 4.5 million years ago, and it then passed on to *Homo habilis* 2 million years ago, then to *Homo erectus* 1.6 million years ago, to *Homo sapiens arcaicus* 250,000 years ago, and it finally reached its apex with *Homo sapiens sapiens* 150,000 years ago. From this last kind, with its completely reflective consciousness, we are direct descendants.

We now know the levels of this kind of consciousness and its capacity to store information about the evolutionary process. This means that the human consciousness carries marks of the great primordial explosion, of the heat of the explosions of the great red stars that threw heavy materials all over the universe; it preserves memories of the circumvolutions of our galactic, solar and planetary systems, of the pains of the labour in the formation of our common home, the Earth; it keeps within itself the signs of the devastating violence of the dinosaurs, of the unifying capacity of the first brains in reptiles, of the tenderness of the first mammals, of the joys of sociability of our ancestral anthropoids;* it recalls the light of the first act of the understanding, of the creativity of the speech that gives order to the world, and lastly of the great joyful dreams of affection and of living together, as well as of the fears in the face of the threats of the environment and of the fight for survival. The good and traumatizing experiences of the relationship with parents, with man and woman, with birth, pain and death, with the Sun, the Moon and the stars, with the magnificence of the starry sky, have left sources in the human soul, fountainheads whose force of action are still present to this day. These are our ancestral and current memories.

In a certain way, every thing, everything is safeguarded in the human consciousness as a form of memory (subatomic, atomic, mineral, vegetable, animal, human), in the archetypes, dreams, visions, symbols, passions and motions that inhabit our interior. We are carriers of angels and demons, of sym-bolic forces that liven us up towards unity and cooperation, and of dia-bolic forces that divide and destroy our stability.[12]

But the human being is a bearer of freedom and of responsibility. Freedom is present in the human being as the capacity to mould this ancestral material and the world around itself. Freedom endows the human being with the potential to decide whether to cultivate the good angels or the interior demons. It is necessary for the human being to create a right measure of equilibrium by making use of the energies of these angels and demons and then to put this right measure to the service of a project that is in synchrony with those aspects of synergy and cooperation in the universe. This is the human being's chance for either happiness or tragedy.

To care for our whole soul is an immense challenge: care for the feelings, the dreams, desires, contradictory passions, imagination, visions and Utopias that are kept hidden inside the heart. How to tame these forces so that they become constructive and not destructive? Under which sense of life do we put all these dimensions together? Care is the pathway and it offers a direction to be followed.

Care for our spirit, the great dreams of God

The human being body–soul has a particularity; that is, it can feel itself part of the universe and connected to the universe, and it can understand itself as the son or daughter of the Earth, as a being of extreme questioning, responsible for its acts and for the common future that it holds with the Earth. The human being cannot ignore questions which without doubt come to him or her: Who am I? What is my place among the myriads of beings? What is the meaning of being thrown into this tiny planet Earth? Where does the entire universe come from? Who is hidden behind the course of the stars? What can we hope for beyond life and death? Why do we cry at the death of our relatives and friends and feel this to be a dramatic event with no return?

Well, to raise such questions is proper for a being that possesses spirit. Spirit is that moment of the human being body–soul in which it listens to this questioning and seeks to give answers. It is not important how this is done: if through mythological stories, if through drawings on the walls of caves, such as the Cro-Magnon Cave in southern France and the grottos of São Raimundo Nonato in the Brazilian state of

Piauí, in the northeast of Brazil, or if through sophisticated philosophical systems, religious rites or empirical scientific knowledge. The human being as a communicative and questioning being is a spiritual being.

There is another point that is also connected to the spirit dimension. That is, the capacity that the human being possesses to continuously ascribe meaning and to create symbols. The human being is not content only with facts. In facts, the human being discerns values and meanings. The human being listens to things, which are always more than merely things, because these things transform themselves into potential messages to be decoded. Let me give here some examples of this.

In the face of the Amazon River we become completely fascinated, we undergo a majestic experience. When we penetrate the forest we contemplate its unique biodiversity and we become terrified in the face of its immensity, which is depicted in trees, waters, animals, and sounds of various pitches; we undergo an experience of majesty. In the face of this majesty we feel ourselves to be a fragile and meaningless animal, and this causes us to feel afraid and to feel a silent respect, and here we undergo the experience of limitation and of threat.

When we live the fascination of love, we undergo the experience of absolute value, which is capable of transfiguring everything; we turn the loved one into a deity, we transform sunshine into a waterfall of gold and we change the difficulties of work into a pleasurable task.

When we see the supplicant hand of a starving child, we are taken by compassion and we show great generosity. All these experiences are expressions of the spirit that we are.

But there is an experience that has been witnessed since the beginnings of humanity, the experience of the Numinous and of the Divine in the Universe, in life and in the human interior.[13] Why can we not recognize that behind the laws of nature there is a supreme Legislator? Why not accept that in the harmony of the heavens there is the action of an infinite Wisdom? Why not admit that the existence of the universe requires a Creator?

The human being calls this supreme Reality by a thousand names, or simply gives it the name of God. The human being feels that God burns inside in the form of a presence that accompanies human beings and that helps the human being to discern between good and evil. The life force drives the human being to grow, to work, to face challenges, to reach its aims and to live with hope. This force is in the human being, but it is bigger than the human being. It is not within the powers of the human being to manipulate it, to create it or to destroy it. The human being finds itself at its mercy. Is not this a sign of the presence of God in the interior of the human being?[14]

The human being can cultivate the space of the Divine, it can open itself to a dialogue with God, it can trust God with the destiny of life and find in God the meaning of death. It is in this way that spirituality gives origin to religions, which are expressions of the encounter with God within the codes of different cultures.

The sages of all peoples have always preached that unless it cultivates the spiritual space, the human being will feel unhappy and sick and will discover itself to be a thirsty wanderer in search of a source that is not to be found anywhere; but if the human being welcomes the spirit and that which inhabits itself then the human being will fill itself up with light, serenity and with imperishable happiness.

To care for the spirit means to care for the values that guide our life and for the meanings that provide hope for beyond our death. To care for the spirit implies to put ethical commitments above personal and collective interests. Care for the spirit demands feeding the internal fire of contemplation and of prayer so that it never goes out. It means in particular to care for spirituality by experiencing God in all and by allowing God's birth and rebirth in the heart. Only in this way can we prepare ourselves with serenity and joviality for the ultimate crossing and for the great encounter.

Care for the great crossing, death

Entropy* is present everywhere, including in the fabric of our lives where it is present until the moment when it consumes all energy resources, and then we die. This is the period of the human being as body. But what happens with the human being as soul–spirit? What about its destiny? This takes a different route. When the human being as soul–spirit appears in this world it starts to be born, it continues to be born, until it finishes being born.

A careful existential analysis reveals the presence of two paths in human existence; that is, the path of the human being as body and the path of the human being as soul–spirit.

The path of the human being as body follows this course: it is born, it grows, it matures, it ages and dies. Death does not come from the outside. It is rather part of the process of life; it is the progressive loss of the vital force.

The other path, the path of the human being as soul–spirit, follows the opposite trajectory. It is born, it starts as a small sign and blossoms, fulfils its potentials, such as being able to speak, to establish relations, to love, and so on. It continues to be born until it finishes being born.

But when does it finish being born? When the two existential paths cross. When they cross real death occurs.

What is the meaning of death? For the human being as body it represents the period of the journey through this spatial–temporal world. For the human being as soul–spirit it represents the possibility of a complete realization of its latent dynamics that were not allowed to emerge due to the constraints of time and space. The death of the human being as body has the function of bringing down barriers. It is in this way that the human being as soul–spirit frees itself of all its constraints

113

and that its interior impulse can realize itself following the logic of the infinite. The intelligence that only saw within the light–dark context now sees in complete light; the will that felt itself conditioned now bursts out in an immediate communion with the object of desire; the essential care that was exercised with ambiguities now finds itself in its complete authenticity; the body that allowed us to enter into communion with and to distance ourselves from others now feels as an expression of our complete union with the totality of the cosmos.

In death, thus, the true birth of the human being occurs. The human being implodes and explodes into its complete identity. Christianity calls this moment of absolute realization 'resurrection'. Resurrection is much more than the reanimation of the corpse and the return to the previous life. Resurrection is the complete realization of the potentialities that are present in the human being. The apostles witnessed such a blessed event with Jesus of Nazareth after his death on the cross. It is for this reason that Jesus is presented as the 'new Adam' (1 Corinthians 15.45), the new creature that touched the end of time. Jesus is the real symbol that the human being can definitely be born.[15]

According to this perspective we do not live to die. We die to resurrect, to live more and better. Death stands for the metamorphosis into this new mode of being in plenitude. When it dies, the human being leaves behind itself a corpse. It is like the cocoon that contained the chrysalis. The cocoon falls off and a radiant butterfly emerges, life in its complete identity. It is resurrection already in death.

The meaning that we give to life is dependent on the sense that we ascribe to death. If death is the final end then so much effort, commitment and sacrifice have little value. But if death is the end-reached-goal then it means a pilgrimage to the fountain. Death belongs to life and it represents the wise way in which life reaches a plenitude that is denied to it in this universe, which is too small for its impulses and extremely narrow for its longing for the infinite. Only the Infinite can quench its infinite thirst.

To care for our great crossing is to internalize our hopeful understanding of death. It is to cultivate our desire of the Infinite by preventing it from being identified with finite objects. It is to meditate, to contemplate and to love the Infinite as our real Object of desire. It is to believe that when we die we will fall into the arms of the Infinite, in an endless embrace and in an infinite and eternal communion. In short it is to undergo the experience of the mystics: the life of love transformed in the Loved.

10

Pathologies of care

Everything that is straight can be bent. By the fact that it is simultaneously *sapiens* (rational) and *demens* (irrational) the human being lives a structural ambiguity. Its good is never entirely good. Its evil is never totally bad. Good and evil, symbolic and dia-bolic, madness and wisdom, essential care and fatal carelessness are blended together. This situation is, in its totality, unbearable. We must approach it realistically. We must neither cry nor rejoice over it. We must learn the lessons that it reveals to us.

Certainly the first lesson is the following: we must be compassionate with ourselves. For the more that we try to correct ourselves there will always be some distortions left, and it is important for us to accept these with some humour and joviality.

Some people are obsessed with being perfectly virtuous. They torture themselves, they terrorize other people and continually spoil their good moods because they are faced, at each moment, with their own limitations and failures.

Wise was the philosopher Immanuel Kant who, in 1784, wrote in his book *Idea for a Universal History from a Cosmopolitan Point of View*: 'Out of such a crooked material as man is made of nothing can be hammered quite straight.'[1] This is the human condition! It is appropriate therefore to accept one's own limitations with humility and without lamentation. In their totality these limitations are insurmountable. We are beings of incompleteness. We are not God.

Once this fact is acknowledged, some give up and stop searching for an improvement of the human condition. They surrender themselves to the gravity that pulls down and to the convenience of going downhill. These are generally people who are sad because they have lost the enthusiasm and the lightness of life. Giving up is just a step away from cynicism.

From this we can learn a second lesson: the fact that we always carry with us a shadow of carelessness does not stop us from a constant pursuit of essential care. Carelessness, which is inherent in the human condition, is more than an obstacle; it is a challenge, leading to living with essential care and with its alternative and more perfect forms. To care is not a goal to be reached at the end of the journey. It is a principle that accompanies the human being at each step, at each moment, along the whole of earthly life, as it was established by Saturn in the fable-myth of Hyginus. Therefore, it is always possible to grow with the practice of care in each instance along life's journey. Such an attitude will generate some quiet happiness and will provide some lightness to the gravity of life.

The negation of essential care

Just as the worst disease is the negation of existence, in a similar way, the worst aberration of care is its negation. As a consequence of this negation the human being devotes itself to the logic of the destructive way-of-being through work, to the hunger for power without limits, to the kind of self-affirmation that leads to the exclusion of the other, and to the bad treatment of people, of the home, of the community and of the person itself. Here we are presented with the human being withdrawing into the limits of its own horizons through the negation of the essence of its being through care, and in doing this the human being becomes cruel to itself. The outcome of this is a process of dehumanization and brutalization of relations. It is equivalent to the theological category of hell, where relationship is denied and the capacity to feel compassion and love is drowned. In biblical terms this is also referred to as the abomination of desolation. Once this situation takes a hold, everything, effectively, is possible, even the impossible.

Care in excess: obsession

There are those who take care in excess. It is a nuisance. The person becomes too obsessed with taking care of everyone and everything. 'The excesses of truth', said Pascal, 'are worse than error.' In a similar way one cannot be concerned with care only. Care is the essence of the human being, but the human being is not its essence only. There is also the meandering human being's history, the resonances of care, and the limitations that need to be accepted and pardoned.

It is in speech that the obsessed shows itself continuously. The obsessed says at every moment: 'Be careful . . . be careful . . . be careful!' So much care ends up suppressing the spontaneity of people who feel themselves continuously embarrassed and robbed of the energy to undergo the experience of essential care, and the trials and errors that are involved with it.

Excess of care for oneself gives rise to narcissism, vanity and affectation. Some people spend hours in front of the mirror. They take care of their acne problem with the same effort as if they were taking care of the course of the stars. Others are so careful with everything they do that they are always late; they lose track of time and irritate people who feel themselves robbed of their own time.

Excess of care causes an immobilizing perfectionism. There are those who put so much care into everything that they never finish what they have started. They lose unique opportunities, profitable situations and possibilities for growth. It is no wonder that these people always feel unsatisfied, putting things on top of things and adding details on top of details. They become ultimately immobilized.

The lack of care: carelessness

There are those who lack in care. These are the careless and the negligent. Usually, these people cannot put themselves entirely into things. This may be because they have lost their stability, because they have taken on too many things to do, or because they do not put all their effort in the things that they do. Things appear to be badly done, spurned, not in order, confused and chaotic; in short, uncared for. The person becomes impatient and loses his or her calm and serenity.

I have argued that care emerges when the right measure is established. This is the middle ground between the way-of-being through work as an activity of exploitation and the way-of-being through care as an activity of providing form. For this reason, care admits neither excesses nor deficiencies. Care is the ideal point of equilibrium between excesses and deficiencies.

The human task is to build this equilibrium with self-control and moderation and, more importantly, with the help of the Spirit of life who never fails because, according to a medieval hymn which is sung to this day in the liturgy of Pentecost, 'Rest art Thou in our toil, most sweet refreshment in the noonday heat; and solace in our grief.'[2] The Spirit of life is dynamic equilibrium.

11

Exemplary figures of care

The way-of-being through care is only truly convincing when it becomes a saga in the biography of people and shapes existential circumstances.

The care of our mothers and grandmothers

Some people concentrate and radiate care in a very special manner: our mothers and the mothers of our mothers, our grandmothers. It is not necessary here to go into too much detail about this experience. This is a central experience for each person since the first thing that a child comes to know is its own mother. To be a mother is more than a mere function, it is a way-of-being that encompasses all dimensions of the woman–mother: her body, her psyche and her spirit. With her care and tenderness the mother continues to vitalize her sons and daughters throughout life. Even if her children have died they will remain in her maternal heart. In dangerous moments mothers are invoked as a reference of assurance and salvation. It is through our mothers that each one of us learns to be mothers to ourselves as we learn to accept ourselves, to forgive our own weaknesses, and as we feed the dream of a great Womb that welcomes everyone. Mothers also represent the way-of-being mother to educators who devote themselves to the improvement of the human being and to the mental and spiritual improvement of their pupils, to nurses who take care of the sick and other people who selflessly devote themselves to the care of someone.

Jesus, a being of care

Jesus of Nazareth, alongside the Buddha, is one of the religious figures that most personify the way-of-being through care. He revealed to humankind the caring God experienced as divine Father and Mother who cares for each hair on our heads, the birds' food, and the sun and the rain for all (cf. Luke 21.18, Matthew 5.45). Jesus showed essential care for the poor, the hungry, the excluded and the sick. He was filled with compassion and cured many. In an unprecedented way for the time, Jesus connected to himself in friendship with various women as disciples (Luke 8.2–3). He cultivated a tender love for his friends Martha and Mary (John 11.20–8; Luke 10.38–42). He did not distance himself from the signs of erotic love demonstrated by a publicly sinful woman who kissed and anointed his feet with ointment (Luke 7.37–9).

He made mercy the key for his ethic. It is through mercy that human beings arrive at the kingdom of life; without mercy there is no salvation for anyone (Matthew 25.36–41). The parables of the good Samaritan who showed compassion for the man who had fallen in a road (Luke 10.30–7), and of the prodigal son who was welcomed and forgiven by his father (Luke 15.11–32) are exemplary expressions of care and of complete humanity.

While dying on the cross, Jesus cares for the two robbers who were crucified alongside him, and he also cares for his mother whom he leaves to the care of his favourite disciple John (John 19.26–7). Jesus was a being of care. The evangelist Mark said with extreme understanding: 'He has done all things well; he even makes the deaf hear and the dumb speak' (Mark 7.37). Jesus cared for the totality of life.

Francis of Assisi: the affection of the universal sibling

In the Western tradition, Francis of Assisi (1182–1226) is seen as an exemplary figure of great importance. Everything in his life is woven into extreme care for nature, for animals, for birds and plants, for the poor and especially for his friend and follower, Clare of Assisi.

With an acute perception he felt the fraternal and sororal ties of affection that unite all beings. With tenderness he called everything brother or sister: the sun, the moon, the ants and the wolf of Gubbio. Everything has a heart. He felt their beat and nourished veneration and respect for every being, even the smallest ones. In the vegetable patch, even the weed has its place because even it praises God.

Biographers of the age, such as the brothers Thomas of Celano and St Bonaventure, witnessed the impact of such gentleness. They say that Francis 'recovered the original innocence', that he 'is the new man given to the world by the heavens', and that, finally, he represents 'the evangelist of our times'. In fact, in the face of the problems of the current state of affairs of ecology worldwide we can recognize his relevance for the present day. We have lived long and we are still attached to the way-of-being through work as the domination of and aggression against nature. St Francis, however, is a true alternative because of his radical way of being care with respect, veneration and affection towards all things.

In a manuscript of the convent of Monte Alverno, where St Francis received the signs of the stigmata, his final farewell to all creatures was preserved. He was very sick and about to die. He bid farewell to Friar Masseo, to Brother Cliff and to Brother Falcon. Then he said: *'Io mio parto da voi con la persona, ma vi lascio il mio cuore.'* That is, 'I depart from you as a person but I leave you my heart.' Indeed, the heart of Francis stands for a style of life, for the inspired expression of care, the practice of confraternity and a renewed fascination for the world. Recreating this heart in people and rescuing cor-diality in relations can arouse in today's world the same appreciation for the symphony of the universe and the same care for the Sister and Mother Earth as was exemplarily lived by St Francis.

Mother Teresa of Calcutta: the principle of mercy

Without doubt, the Catholic nun Mother Teresa of Calcutta (1910–97) was one of the living archetypes of essential care. She was born in Albania but worked from 1928 in India as a missionary and as a teacher in a day school. Everything went according to plan until 1946 when, while travelling by train, she said that she heard a clear voice telling her to leave the convent and to help and live among the poor. She understood this to be a divine call. When she was 38 years old she left the convent, changed her heavy black robe for a practical and cheap cotton sari, and went to live in a shack in the impoverished suburbs of Calcutta, living on a diet of rice and salt like the poor, to help the poor. When followers started to join her she founded the Order of the Missionaries of Charity. She imposed a fourth vow beyond the three vows of poverty, obedience and chastity, that is, to 'give wholehearted and free service to the poorest of the poor.'

In Calcutta there are thousands and thousands of impoverished people who are born, live and die on the streets. Mother Teresa soon founded the Home for the Dying. She rescued the dying from the streets and took them to the home so that they could die with dignity. It was here that a labour of compassion and mercy began, which spread out to many cities in India, Pakistan and other countries – a labour that always aimed at providing dignity and humanity to those who are dying.

The Order of the Missionaries of Charity cultivates a charisma that is directly linked to the tenderness of life, the charisma of touching people, touching their skin, their bodies, their wounds. 'Touch them, wash them, feed them,' said Mother Teresa constantly to the sisters and to the many volunteers who came from all over the world to help her work. At other times she said, 'Give Christ to the world, do not keep him for yourselves, and when you do it use your hands.' Her biographer Anne Sebba commented: 'The ability to touch, with its wider implications, is especially important in India where the concept of "untouchability" is so real. This is the true missionary spirit in action; it is more important to touch than to cure.'[1] The hand that touches, heals because it caresses; it brings back trust, it offers acceptance and it manifests care. The hand generates the human essence in those who are touched.

In 1979 Mother Teresa received the Nobel Peace Prize. And she gave it its true meaning by saying: 'I accept the prize in the name of the poor. The prize is the recognition of the poor of the world.'

Many have questioned the efficacy of the work of Mother Teresa. Instead of tackling the circumstances that cause someone to die on the streets, these critics say, she only takes care of the victims and as such she perpetuates their miserable condition. They ask: Should we care for or should we free the poor? I answer: We must do both things because both things make sense. Mother Teresa had discovered her path to essential care and as such she answered the question with a slight smile: 'While you talk about the causes and the implications, I kneel down beside the poorest of the poor and I take care of their needs.'

One strategy does not invalidate the other. There is a bare minimum of humanity that must always be protected; this is to save lives in the face of the imminence of death. This is not a form of assistance; it is basic humanism without which we become cynical and merciless. For this reason it is always appropriate to give bread to those who feel hunger, for hunger does not wait. Mother Teresa noted well: 'The people who reach me are sick and dying; they are so weak that they cannot even hold a fishing hook; we must first give to them the fish and perhaps later the fishing hook.' Even so it is always important to tackle the structural causes, to help change society so that no one has to die abandoned on a street. Both strategies are the outcome of com-passion and of essential care: one strategy uses the hand to reach people, the other uses a long embrace reaching the structures.

Others criticized Mother Teresa's naivety in accepting help from people who are clearly oppressors, such as the dictator Duvalier of Haiti or the North American millionaire Charles Keating who defrauded millions of dollars from savings and loans accounts. I think the following regarding this issue: the world of Mother Teresa was a world of goodness without a stain, and far from any form of malice or opportunism. What she saw was not the hand that gave but the sick and the dying who need help. Everything that could help recover their dignity as people made sense for her and became justified, without legitimizing the personal ambiguities of the donors.

She was used by the ecclesiastical apparatus many times to publicize in world forums the official thesis about birth control, about their condemnation of abortion and about the denial of orders to women. Such orthodox views could not be further away from her day-to-day practices, but she obediently put herself forward to defend those views.

In spite of all these limitations Mother Teresa radiated exemplary compassion and warm care towards the most impoverished of the poor. Her figure is a call from the attitude of the good Samaritan who bends over the fallen on the street. More than medicines, it is this attitude of essential care that cures and rescues wounded humanity.

Brother Antônio: a hunter of smiles in sad faces

Just as important as bringing dignity to the death of those who die on the streets is to bring dignity to the life of those who live on the streets, those who drink, who are sick and who have been abandoned. This is exactly what Brother Antônio Mendes de Ferreira tries to do in the city of Petrópolis in the interior of the state of Rio de Janeiro, Brazil. In a similar way, many other people work with street kids, lonely elderly people and terminally ill patients.

The figure of Brother Antônio, despite his personal limitations, radiates an amazing aura of goodness and reverence. He was born in Portugal and was a sailor for many years. The routes through the oceans and the silence of the seas, he says, deepened his insatiable search for happiness. He did not find it in any harbour in which his ship set anchor. After reflecting a good deal and asking for enlightenment from God he understood: 'Happiness is the fruit of my gift to the other; my gift is only true if it can bring a smile to a sad face.'

In one port he found someone who was in such a miserable state that it caused him to feel repugnance. However, he approached this person. They began talking. And then, suddenly, the beggar gave a wonderful smile because of his talk with Brother Antônio. This was enough to provoke in Brother Antônio an indescribable happiness. He discovered the key to a happy life; that is, to care for those who are condemned and rejected on the streets and, in his own words, 'become a hunter for smiles in sad faces'.

To better achieve this he took orders with the Ordem de São João de Deus, or Order of St John of God, a Portuguese saint from the end of the fifteenth century who in Granada in Spain served the poorest of the street, especially Muslims who were discriminated against by Christians.

Some time after, Brother Antônio went to Brazil to serve the poor there. He associated himself with the then recently created Pastoral do Homem de Rua in Petrópolis. He gave shelter to the impoverished people living on the streets, provided them with hot soup and a place to sleep. It did not take too long for him to come into conflict with religious institutions. On one occasion, a drunk man from the street asked him for a bath. He took the drunk man to his community but his superior forbade it. He went to another convent, and to another, and to another, and all of them closed their doors to them. He continued to insist that the impoverished of the streets should be allowed to have a bath at least once in a while. And as he insisted on this small thing from the religious institutions, which are committed to the vow of poverty, and as he was never granted this he ended up being advised to leave the Ordem de São João de Deus.

He changed his base but he did not abandon the fight. Alone, he worked the whole day on the streets, welcoming beggars, gathering drunkards, and taking them to a warehouse in the Rua 24 de Maio where they could have a bath, shave, change their clothes, have some hot soup and spend the night. His objective was and is 'to seek to dignify those who are fallen in the street'.

Later the place became the Acolhimento São João de Deus, a very basic refuge but open to all. People are not required to complete forms or present identification. They arrive, have a bath and sleep. It is the home of the condemned of the streets.

With the help of the impoverished of the streets themselves, who gradually stopped drinking, a movement was organized to help beggars to find work. The Hospedaria Bento Meni was built to achieve this. There they can live and have the minimum infrastructure such as sanitation, running water and electricity. For those who want to change and work on the land, a small farm in Brejal, close to the outskirts of Petrópolis, was acquired. There children, adults and the elderly live, cultivate vegetables and take care of livestock.

Brother Antônio's work is supported only by the good will of the people and nobody else. With the support he received he built a sizeable warehouse in the suburbs of Petrópolis, where he organized the Grupo de Reciclagem Emaús. Everything that is brought to it, such as paper, plastic, bottles, unwanted things, is put to good use and recycled so that it can be reused by local enterprises. Many beggars and men and women of the streets work there, going and coming, earning enough for their basic needs. The dream now is to build the

Aldeia Hospitaleira, a small development with 50 houses to accommodate those who want to start a new life. The imperial family[2] of Petrópolis has donated a good piece of land to this end, and three houses have been built on it already.

Dignity, says Brother Antônio, is achieved only if we give value to the populations of the streets. To give value is to welcome them with goodwill, to listen to their lamentations, touch them and embrace them so that they can recover their self-esteem. When the skin touches another's skin it allows the rebirth of the humanity that has been lost.

When they gather together, Brother Antônio states quite clearly: 'We are here not so much to make something, but to be together, to re-establish the lost links with our humanity, to share together our things, our ideas and our dreams.' And when the humiliated and offended listen to this they are filled with emotion because they pray for their desires and celebrate their dreams and, at the same time, lament their failures and cry because of the exclusion they suffer from a merciless society.

This work does not aim solely to provide basic needs but, more importantly, to instigate discipline and to rescue the value of personal autonomy. It always seeks to unite the elderly with the abandoned children. It starts from the following observation: children need love and the elderly have a lot of love to give and care to receive. One complements the other and as such their relationship produces a humanizing effect that is incalculable to the children who feel that they are being supported and to the elderly who feel themselves to be useful and loved.

The care that Brother Antônio devotes to the poor and to their being granted dignity is fed by a mystic of solidarity. His motto is taken from St Paul: 'I have become all things to all men, that I might by all means save some' (1 Corinthians 9.22). But he does not bring religion into the space of the poor; he intends to humanize them, and the religious baggage carried by each one of them is a humanizing, efficient and integrative resource that he knows to approach with respect and care in the form of prayer, of thanksgiving and of cheerful celebrations. Once more, it is essential care that encourages this libertarian work with the poorest of the poor so that they can not only die humanly but also live with some dignity.

Mahatma Gandhi: the politics of care with the people

A figure who had a great impact in the twentieth century is without a doubt Mahatma Gandhi (1869–1948). He was born in India, graduated in law in London and worked for more than 20 years in South Africa (1893–1915), defending the rights of Indian immigrants, who were victims of racial segregation. While in Africa he came into contact with the ideals propagated by Leo Tolstoy (1883–1945), the author of *War and Peace* and *Anna Karenina*. Tolstoy saw the essence of the message of Jesus in the Sermon of the Mount, in love, in the rejection of all violence, in revering the poor and in the commitment to a simple life. Such ideals deeply impressed Gandhi and helped him to formulate his own vision of non-violence and of political engagement with care for the people. Gandhi even founded a rural community called 'Tolstoy', where he tried to live these ideals with friends.

On returning to India he devoted himself to the task of organizing the people against British domination. He started to argue for the boycott of British produce, especially textiles. He encouraged the rescue of the old familiar tradition of weaving garments at home. He invoked people to civil disobedience. He was arrested numerous times. His march to the sea is famous. By force of a decree from the colonizers the Indians could buy only salt that was taxed by the British. Gandhi mobilized thousands and thousands of people, who marched in the direction of the sea to extract the salt they needed. He was arrested but he achieved the complete liberation of the salt industry.

Gandhi defined politics as 'a loving gesture towards the people'; in other words, politics with care for the well-being of all and essential tenderness for the poor. He confessed: 'I entered into politics for loving the life of the weak; I lived with the poor, I received pariahs as guests, I have fought so that they would have the same political rights we do, I defied kings and I have forgotten how many times I have been arrested.'

Two basic principles guide this practice; that is, the force of truth (*satuagraha*) and active non-violence (*ahimsa*). Gandhi strongly believed that truth has an invincible force in itself, a force against which manipulation, violence, weapons and prisons are ineffective. He held the profound conviction that behind conflicts lies a latent truth. The function of the politician is to believe in this truth, to bring it to the surface and to all, and to act in accordance with this truth, being willing to endure the sacrifices that such a position requires. He firmly believed that truth, even if late, always wins.

His belief in the force of truth led him to the concept of active non-violence (*ahimsa*), which does not mean to fold one's arms and sit back, but to use all possible peaceful means to achieve one's envisaged objectives. It is important that the means and the ends have the same nature. Good ends demand good means. Active non-violence can be practised, for instance, by occupying the streets, by organizing mass rallies, by fasting and praying, and by offering one's own body against violence. Gandhi criticized the attitude of Denmark, which, in the face of the Nazi invasion, capitulated. The duty of the soldiers, according to Gandhi, was to offer resistance with their own disarmed bodies. The meaning of active non-violence is not to guarantee the victory of one of the sides, but to value the truth that helps build a social power based on equal participation, in collaboration and solidarity with all.

Gandhi elaborated a small creed in the form of a prayer which was recited every day: 'I shall not fear anyone on earth; I shall fear only God; I shall not bear ill will toward anyone; I shall not submit to injustice from anyone; I shall conquer untruth by truth; and in resisting untruth, I shall put up with all suffering.'

Gandhi was a very religious person. He knew Christianity well and had a great veneration for Jesus. But he continued with Hinduism since he believed that all religions, at heart, catch and express the same divine truth. He was a firm believer that prayer and fasting could help change political situations. For this reason every time there was a major political deadlock he put himself to prayer and to fasting for weeks, and he invited the masses to do the same. He made the British Empire tremble and he talked opposing forces out of their opposing views.

He possessed a deep concern for all beings. As a commandment he preached: 'You shall love the smallest of the creatures as you love yourself. Whoever does not practise this will never see the face of God.' He sought to live in harmony with all living beings. For this reason he gave up meat altogether, and cow's milk, which he understood to be obtained by violent means. He drank only goat's milk, which he himself had milked. Through his sparse diet and fasting he desired to render reverence to life, as if he was saying to all things: 'You can rest calm; I shall not cause unnecessary suffering to you; I shall only take the minimum necessary for my body to live well.'

Thanks to Gandhi's efforts, India gained her independence from British domination on 15 August 1947. Because of religious conflicts between Hindus and Muslims the country was divided in two: India (of Hindu religion) and Pakistan (of Muslim religion). The divide continues to this day. Gandhi, the messiah of non-violence, was the victim of violence. On 30 January 1948 a fanatical Brahmin murdered him. Gandhi received from the people the title of Mahatma, which means Great Soul.

Clearly, Mahatma Gandhi left to humanity an everlasting legacy; that is, it is possible to unite personal holiness with libertarian political engagement. This personal holiness, which is founded in the passion for truth and in opting for peaceful means, turns politics into something that is more than the mere exercise of public power; politics becomes the loving care for life and an ethical commitment to the destiny of the people as a whole.

The care of Olenka and Tania: the hospitality that saves

Hospitality is par excellence the virtue of nomads, migrants and pilgrims. In a certain way we are all pilgrims since we are travelling through the paths of life and very often we find ourselves meeting strangers, who deserve our hospitality. Without hospitality, people, communities and entire populations do not encourage reciprocity among themselves and do not reinforce peace and friendship between them either.

Hospitality can be understood as an expression of care. There are moments in which this form of care transformed into hospitality saves people who have been threatened. It was exactly this that happened to the Romanian Jew Michael Stilveman, who is now a Brazilian citizen and who has lived in Rio de Janeiro as a businessman since 1948.

In his book *A Marcha* he narrates the perverse way in which the Nazis in Romania eliminated Jews. They forced the Jews to walk with no destination, day and night, while being despised and stoned until the moment when they fell dead through fatigue and hunger.

Stilveman, at the age of 13, was forced to take part in this sinister march. He narrates the facts of this great barbarity and treason and, at the same time, of moving hospitality. After marching for three months non-stop he was half-dead, but he managed to escape with his mother, who was dying. They were rescued by a villager called Olenka and her daughter Tania, who risked their own lives to save the threatened life of strangers. They gave Stilveman and his mother their first bath in months, they cared for their wounds, they shared their scanty provisions, and they gave up their own beds to them.

Olenka and Tania revealed the human essence of care and compassion. Because of their deep humanity they will be forever remembered. More than giving back Stilveman and his mother physical strength, they gave them back the fundamental trust in the goodness of life. In spite of recurring aberrations life follows a sacred path and it is worthwhile to live it with care and compassion.

The prophet of the principle of kindness

Each age has its prophets who reveal, announce, console and keep the light of hope alive. In the first chapter of this book I stated that our age is characterized by the stigma of the lack of care and by the loss of kindness in personal and social relations. This stigma affects mainly the great urban conglomerations. For example, Rio de Janeiro is a city in which natural kindness is generously shown in the scenery through the ecological composition of the sea, mountains and forests, and in which a human kindness is also shown through a population that is easy-going and full of good humour. But gradually it saw social relations being brutalized by violence against street kids, by frequent crimes and by the stress caused by traffic. Within this context a man appeared, José da Trino (1917–96), who started to preach to the city and humanity that kindness is an alternative way of living. He had a major impact on the popular strata of society, who started to call him 'Prophet Kindness'.

Like any true prophet within a determined historical context, he also felt a divine call. He owned a small road haulage company in the northern part of the city of Rio de Janeiro, in Guadalupe. He led a normal life, just like any worker from the popular strata of society, until 17 December 1961 when the Gran Circus Norte Americano caught fire in Niterói, on the far side of the Bay of Guanabara, opposite Rio. Four hundred people were burned to ashes. Such a tragedy affected José da Trino. Six days after this event the prophetic vocation emerged in him, between the hours of midday and 1 p.m., when he was delivering goods with his lorry. He himself acknowledged that he had received a divine call, confirmed three times, that he must leave everything behind and devote himself to consoling the victims of the circus in Niterói. On Christmas Eve he took his lorry and bought two 100-litre barrels of wine and went to Niterói. There, alongside the ferry crossing, he started to distribute wine in paper glasses to everybody, and he announced: 'Whoever wants to drink some wine does not need to pay; it is enough to say please . . . and to say thank you.'

After this he stayed for four years where the fire had taken place. He fenced the area in and transformed it into a garden full of flowers. He put up two gates, one to serve as the entrance and the other as the exit, with the inscription: 'Welcome to the Paradise of Kindness. Come in, do not smoke, and do not swear because this has now become a holy field.'

He consoled all of those who arrived feeling desperate by saying: 'Your father, your mother, your daughter, your son did not die; the body has died, the spirit has not. God has made his call. Even the worst sinner has been saved because God is not vengeful . . . I have been sent by God and I came to console you.' In fact, those who came and heard his message left feeling better.

Curiously, just as with the biblical prophets, the Prophet Kindness foresaw in these events the manifestation of a deeper meaning. The circus suggested the world as a circus, as a theatre and representation. Its destruction was a metaphor for the destruction of a world built on the lack of kindness and charity. He said emphatically: 'The remains of a burned circus in Niterói stand for a representation of a particular world . . . the following has happened: the world is round and the circus had a round shape; for this reason, with the fire in the circus that particular world is finished.' The alternative to this world that has been eliminated rests in living with kindness and in the attitude of being grateful.

He took his vocation seriously. He made a white robe, took a staff, and carried a banner full of decorations carrying messages of kindness. He travelled around Brazil, especially in the north and northeast regions, before settling for good in Rio de Janeiro. He went around the city, preached in squares, presented himself to people on the ferries between Rio and Niterói. He always lived among the people.

From 1980 a new phase in his prophetic activity began. He wrote down his teaching on 55 pillars of the Viaduct of Caju at the entrance to the city of Rio. There, he denounced the threats to nature that are caused by, as he said, 'the devil-money'. But the strength of his message was centred on kindness. To express his message he used the code he knew, Christian Trinitarian symbolism. Everything was thought of and announced in the name of the Father, the Son and the Holy Ghost. It is interesting to note here that he did not use only Trinitarian terminology, which is the most common, but also quaternarian terminology, which is very rare. The psychoanalyst C. G. Jung (1875–1961), who studied in depth the symbols of totality, demonstrated that the Christian Trinity did not stand for a doctrine only. It is a code that stands for an integrated totality. For this reason it uses the symbol 3 – Father, Son and Holy Ghost – or the number 4 – Father, Son, Holy Ghost, and Nature or Mary. The fourth element, according to Jung, is always the feminine.

The numbers 3 and 4 should not be understood as mathematical numbers, but as archetypes or numeric symbols that express an experience of totality. The number 3, the totality turned in on itself, and the number 4, the totality turned away from itself, or the sum of 4 plus 3 which is 7, the archetype of a globalization that includes everything – God, the universe, man and woman.

This archetypal symbolism appears quite clearly in the messages of the Prophet Kindness. The universe, for instance, appears written as '*univvverrsso*' (instead of *universo*) to demonstrate the action of the three divine entities (*vvv*), and in particular the Son (*rr*) and the Holy Ghost (*ss*). Love is always thought of in a Trinitarian way. For this reason he writes love as '*amorrr*' (instead of *amor*) and he explains it as: 'material love is written with one r, universal love is written with three rs: one r for the Father, another r for the Son, and yet another r for the Holy Ghost; thus, *amorrr*.' Sometimes he puts along with the Father, the Son and the Holy Ghost, Nature or our Lady (F/S/G/L).[3]

But the guiding principle of everything is kindness, as a way-of-being. Every now and again he announced without tiring: 'Kindness generates kindness.' 'God the Father is kindness that generates the Son through kindness.' He refused to say '*Muito obrigado*' ('I am much obliged', which is the Brazilian Portuguese phrase most commonly used for 'thank you'), because, he argued, one not obliged, in the sense of being forced, to do anything; one should just be kind towards others and relate to others in love. Instead of saying '*Muito obrigado*' we should say '*agradecido*' ('I am grateful'); instead of saying '*Por favor*' ('please') we should say '*Por gentileza*' ('Will you do me the kindness'), because in this way we reconnect ourselves to kindness and to the grace that is God, for he has created everything with kindness and in complete gratuity.

If Pascal, as we have already seen, spoke of the *esprit de finesse*, José da Trino conceived the *esprit de gentillesse* (spirit of kindness) with the same basic sense as Pascal's. The resonances of this spirit are given in the following values which are inscribed on his robe and on the pillars of the viaduct: 'kindness-love-beauty-perfection-goodness-richness-in-nature'. This fountain-head of kindness was not merely preached by him but also lived by him. He treated all with extreme kindness. When people called him mad, he answered: 'Mad to love you, mad to save you' or 'Be mad like me, be a nice madman, mad about nature, mad about things that are divine.'

He realized the importance for the world of the principle of kindness. During RIO 92[4] he begged the representatives of peoples and the heads of state to live in kindness and to apply themselves to the use of kindness.

Feeling ill, he decided to return to his birth place, the town of Cafelândia in the state of São Paulo. He died, however, in the town of Mirandópolis in the state of São Paulo on 28 May 1996 at the age of 79.

Leonardo Guelman, a young Brazilian philosopher, dedicated himself to a detailed work of reconstruction and a philosophical and cultural analysis of the life and message of Prophet Kindness. It is entitled *Univvverrsso Gentileza, a gênese de um mito contemporâneo*. Along with this work he produced a very beautiful CD-ROM disk. The work concludes with the following statement, which is relevant here:

> [The Prophet] Kindness has turned himself towards a way of humanizing life in modern cities. Modern cities, which are marked by violence and by the indifference of their inhabitants, are for the Prophet a world to be restored. It was this that occurred in the place where the circus stood in Niterói and in the viaducts of Caju in Rio de Janeiro. Over the ashes and over the fumes of the viaducts of the megalopolis, in the most inhospitable and desolated places of the megalopolis, the man that came from Cafelândia in the state of São Paulo went to exalt his 'announcement' in blue lettering and in yellow-green banners. It is the perspective of a simple man, a perspective born out of his experience of reality and of Brazilian culture, which establishes itself as a fundamental alternative to a way of life that is harmful to all. 'Kindness generates kindness' proclaims the Prophet in more than half of his writings in Rio de Janeiro.[5]

In the middle of the concrete jungle into which modern cities have been transformed the Prophet announced an ethos that is able to inspire a new paradigm of civilization; that is, spreading kindness as essential care and tenderness. This paradigm has more chance of integrating and of humanizing than the other paradigm which disappeared with the circus in Niterói, the old paradigm of the way-of-being through work-domination.

Feng shui: the Chinese philosophy of care

As a summary of everything I have reflected on thus far I wish to introduce the important topic of the Chinese way of seeing the world, a topic which comes under the name 'feng shui'. In its multiple facets, feng shui represents a final synthesis of care which is concretized in the way in which garden and home are organized, by postulating a level of right measure and of integrating the elements present in a given context. This approach has rarely been seen in other cultures. We could even say here that the Chinese are to the East what the Greeks were for the West; they are the untiring searchers for dynamic equilibrium in all things. From this fact comes the increasing relevance that feng shui is gaining worldwide.

The supreme ideal of Chinese tradition is found in Taoism, of which Lao-tse (sixth century BCE) and Chuang-tsu (fourth century BCE) are the best-known scholars, which consists in searching for unity through a process of integration of differences, especially of the well-known polarities of yin/yang, masculine/feminine, space/time and celestial/terrestrial, among others. The Tao* represents this integration, the integration of an indescribable reality and the person who seeks to unite itself with this reality.

Tao means the path and the method, but it is also the mysterious and secret energy that produces all paths and projects all methods. It cannot be expressed in words, so when in front of it silence is best. It is present in all things as the immanent principle that ascribes meaning. It underlies the yin and the yang and through them it manifests itself. The human ideal is to reach a union with Tao so profound that *satori*, enlightenment, is produced. This union grants us immortality and eternity. For Taoists the supreme good is not reached on the other side, after death, as for Christians; it happens rather within time and history through an experience that is non-dualistic and that causes integration with Tao. When the person dies it unifies itself to Tao.

To reach this union it is imperative to be in synchrony with the vital energy that weaves through the heavens and earth, *chi*. It is impossible to translate *chi*, but it is equivalent to the *ruach* of the Jewish people, to the *pneuma* of the Greeks, to the *spiritus* of the Latins, to the *axé* of the Yoruba/Nago; these are expressions that designate the universal breath, the supreme and cosmic energy.

It is because of *chi* that everything changes and remains in a constant process of change (cf. the book *I Ching* or *The Book of Changes*). It flows through the human being through the meridians of *acupuncture*. It circulates through the earth, through underground telluric veins that are created by those electromagnetic fields distributed along the meridians of *eco-puncture* that criss-cross the surface of the Earth. When *chi* expands itself it signifies life; when it retracts itself it signifies death. When it becomes condensed it represents itself as matter; when it becomes subtle it represents itself as spirit. Nature is the wise combination of *chi* in its various states, from the most condensed to the most light.

Chi takes the form of two archetypal animals in Chinese culture, the tiger and the dragon. These animals stand for rationality and masculinity, the tiger; and for emotion and femininity, the dragon. When they meet in a given place, pleasant scenery emerges, scenery with a light breeze and crystal-clear waters, wavy mountains and luscious green vales. It is an invitation to the human being to install itself there.

The Chinese view of the world privileges space, as opposed to the Western view which privileges time. Space for Taoism is the place of meeting, of living together, of interaction between all and with all, for every thing is a bearer of *chi* energy that fills space. The supreme expression of space realizes itself in the home and the garden. Even in a miniature form they stand for a summary of the universe, of harmonization of the elements, of the symphonic encounter between polarities.

If the human being wants to be happy it must develop *topophilia*, love for the place where one lives and where one builds one's garden. Feng shui is the art and the technique of building one's home and garden well.

What then is feng shui? It literally means 'wind and water'. Originally it was a sage who, through the observation of nature and of a fine synchrony with *chi*, provided the ideal guidelines to build the home and the garden.

Beatriz Bartoly, one of the best commentators on this philosophy in Brazil, writes that:

> Feng shui connects ourselves to a form of affectionate zeal – I would say caring and tender – with the simple things of our existence, an affectionate zeal which in the West has for a long time been discredited and despised: to care for plants and animals, to look after the house, to take care of the cleaning and upkeep of rooms, to prepare food, to adorn everyday life with the prosaic and, at the same time, majestic beauty of nature. However, more important than human construction and building is human conduct and action, and these latter are the main goal of this philosophy of life because for feng shui the process is more important than the outcome. It is the *exercise* of embellishing that is most important and not the beautiful scenery that is achieved through it. The value is in the action and not in the construction; it is in the conduct and not in the building.[6]

As has been demonstrated, feng shui philosophy aims first at the individual, then at the object; at the person, then the environment and the home itself. The person needs to involve him- or herself in the process, to develop a perception of the environment, to pick up the energetic flows and rhythms of nature. The individual must assume a conduct in harmony with others, with the cosmos and with the rhythmic processes of nature. When the individual has created this interior ecology, he or she is capable of successfully organizing the exterior ecology.

More than a science and an art, feng shui is fundamentally an ecological-cosmic ethic of how to take care of the correct distribution of *chi* in our entire environment.

In the face of the dismantling of care and of the current serious ecological crisis, the ancient wisdom of feng shui helps us to reforge the alliance of sympathy and love with nature. This conduct rebuilds the human dwelling with foundations of care and its multiple resonances.

Conclusion: to care and the future of the dispossessed of the earth

The category of care has shown itself to be the deciphering key of human essence. The human being has transcendence and for this reason it breaks taboos, it crosses barriers, and it is content only with the infinite. The human being possesses something of Jupiter inside itself; it is not without reason that it has received spirit from him.

The human being has immanence and for this reason it finds itself placed on a planet, rooted to a place, and moulded within the possibilities of space–time. The human being possesses something of Tellus/Earth inside itself; it is made from the *humus*.

The human being finds itself under the reign of time. Time does not stand for a continuous rush that is empty of content. Time is historic; it runs through the saga of the universe, through human practice, and especially through the struggle of the oppressed who search for life and freedom. Time is constructed step by step and for this reason it is always real, extremely real. But simultaneously, time implies a utopic horizon, a promise of a future plenitude for the human being, for the excluded and for the cosmos. It is only by searching for the impossible that the possible is realized. Due to this dynamic the human being possesses something of Saturn, Lord of Time and Utopia.

But it is not enough to make these points here. These determinations, to tell the truth, tear the human being to pieces. They put the stretched and crucified human being between the heavens and earth, between the present and the future, between injustice and the fight for freedom.

What kind of alchemy will forge the link between Jupiter, Tellus/Earth and Saturn? What energy will articulate transcendence and immanence, history and utopia, the struggle for justice and for peace so that the human being is complete?

The fable-myth of Hyginus transmits to us an ancient wisdom; that is, it is care that binds everything, it is care that brings the heavens into the Earth and that puts the Earth into the heavens, it is care that provides the link from transcendence to immanence, from immanence to transcendence and from history to Utopia. It is care that grants strength to search for peace among the various levels of conflict. Without care that recovers the dignity of a humanity condemned to exclusion, the new paradigm of living together will not be established.

Care comes before spirit (Jupiter) and the body (Tellus). The spirit humanizes itself and the body becomes alive when they are moulded by care. If this was not the case, spirit would lose itself in abstractions and the body would confuse itself with unshaped matter. Care forces spirit to give form to a concrete body that is within time, open to history and adjusted to Utopia (Saturn). It is care that allows the revolution of tenderness when the social is prioritized over the individual and when development is directed towards the improvement of the quality of life of human beings and of other living organisms. Care allows the rise of a human being that is complex, sensitive, compassionate, cordial and connected to everything and everyone in the universe.

Care stamped its mark on every portion, every dimension, every hidden fold of the human being. Without care the human being would become inhuman.

Everything that is alive needs to be fed. In the same way, care, the essence of the human being, also needs to be continuously fed. The resonances of care are care's concrete manifestations in the various forms of existence and, at the same time, they are also care's essential nourishment. Care lives off maternal love, tenderness, caress, compassion, conviviality and the right measure in everything. Without care the human being, like the tamagochi, wastes away and dies.

Today, with the crisis of the human project, we miss the clamorous presence of care everywhere. Its negative resonances are shown through bad quality of life, through the penalizing of an impoverished majority of humanity, through ecological degradation and through the exaltation of violence.

Let us not search for the healing path outside the human being. The ethos is within the human being itself who is to be understood in its completeness that includes the infinite. The human being needs to turn to itself and to rediscover its essence, which is found in care.

Let us pray that care blossoms in every sense, that it penetrates the human sphere and that it prevails in all relationships! Care will save life, it will bring justice to the impoverished and will re-establish the Earth as the fatherland and motherland of all.

Glossary

Androcentrism: a word of Greek origin that designates the centralization of power in the figure of the man (*aner*) and, hence, the domination of women by men.

Animus/anima: concepts disseminated by the psychoanalyst C. G. Jung (1875–1961) to designate the dimensions of the masculine (*animus*) and feminine (*anima*) which are present in every person and which are reflected in cultural patterns of behaviour.

Anthropic principle: a system of ideas based on the following observation: the fact that we are here and that we say all that we say is only possible because the universe formed itself with such a symmetry that it progressed with purpose, reaching its apex in the human being. If this was not the case then we would not be here.

Anthropoid: group of superior primates which includes orang-utans, gorillas and chimpanzees.

Archetype: patterns of behaviour that exist in the collective unconscious of humanity, and which represent basic experiences that aim at guiding life. These archetypes rise to consciousness in the form of great symbols, dreams, Utopias and exemplary figures.

Autopoiesis: self-creation and self-organization of living beings.

Biosphere: everything that lives in the air, on the ground, under the ground and in the water forms the biosphere.

Chaos: unpredictable behaviour in certain systems, especially live systems, which enables a new or different ordering; for this reason it is said that chaos is not 'chaotic' but rather generative.

Co-evolution: the joint evolution of ecosystems with their respective entities, including social and technical systems.

145

Complementarity Principle: a principle put forward by a Danish physicist on Quantum Physics, according to which matter and radiation can be, simultaneously, wave and particle. The two descriptions are complementary. This principle is also applied to other fields where opposites are observed, opposites which are then understood as complementary within the system.

Corporeity: a concept that expresses the totality of the human being while a living being that is part of creation and of nature. It should not be confused with corporality, a dualistic anthropological term that interprets the human being as the union of two distinct parts, the body and the soul.

Cosmology: science that studies the cosmos, its origins, its evolution and its purpose. The idea of the world that a society produces in order to guide itself in the search for knowledge and to locate the place of the human being within the totality of beings.

Cybiont: macroorganism resulting from the *symbiosis* and articulation of the biological with the mechanic and electronic. Modern societies form cybionts since in them human beings, communities, machines and webs of information co-exist and co-evolve forming a whole that is an extension of the evolutionary process, which is now co-piloted by the human being.

Ecosystem: the totality of all systems, be they natural systems or artificial systems, that have been projected by the human being.

Electromagnetic force: force that acts only on particles that possess a charge; if the particles possess opposing charges, they attract each other; if they possess the same charge, they repel each other.

Empowerment: providing power to those without power or the sharing of power between all citizens and the strengthening of active citizenship through social organizations.

Entropy: natural and irreversible dissipation of energy in a closed system; this dissipation tends to zero, and is equivalent to thermic death.

Ethos: in Greek, the burrow of an animal or the human home; collection of principles that govern human behaviour in all cultures, so that it is truly human in the sense of being conscious, free and responsible. The ethos builds the personal and the social in a human habitat (see also *moral*).

Feng shui: Chinese ecological philosophy that seeks to build, in the best possible way, a home or work environment that is considered to be in equilibrium with all energies that act in that particular space.

Fluctuation: the oscillation that occurs in any given order due to the nature of its equilibrium that is always fragile and always to be remade or recreated; living and social systems are always in fluctuation.

Gaia: one of the names given to Earth in Greek mythology. The scientist James Lovelock called Earth the Gaia because it demonstrates reactions and forms of equilibrium that are proper for living beings. As such, it would be a supraorganism that is alive.

Gravitational force: force of attraction that acts on all mass; it is the most universal of the forces, despite being the weakest one.

Hinduism: religion with many branches practised by the majority of Indian peoples; it is the outcome of an ancient evolution of Vedism and Brahminism, which transformed themselves through philosophical enquiry and through integration with local religious systems.

Holism/holistic: derived from the Greek *holos* which means 'totality'. It is the understanding of reality as the articulation of the whole in the parts and of the parts in the whole, for it holds everything to be part of a dynamic, diverse and unique process.

Hominids: group of the primate species that includes the modern human being (*Homo sapiens sapiens*) and its direct ancestors (*Homo sapiens*).

Hyginus: Egyptian slave of Caesar Augustus, then director of the Palatine Library in Rome and author of the fable-myth of essential Care, which is analysed in this book. He died in 10 CE.

Logos: spirit, reason, a meaningful structure, logic.

Matriarchal: see *matrifocal*.

Matrifocal: a culture is described as matrifocal if women (mothers) are at the axis and are the focus of social organization. *Matriarchal* is the opposite of patriarchal.

Moral: the *ethos* realizes itself through the concrete forms of moral, but these morals may differ in different cultures and at different times. All morals, however, are related to the fundamental human ethos, which is only one.

Morphogenic: in the *autopoiesis* of life not only the physico-chemical factors are important but also the singular forms that beings take on, by that which it is able to distinguish itself from other beings within the same and common biological context.

Noosphere: term coined by Teilhard de Chardin to designate a new phase for humanity. This is the phase that comes after the androsphere and the biosphere and is characterized by a global consciousness and a feeling of responsibility for the common destiny that human beings and the planet Earth share together.

Nucleosynthesis: the formation of atomic nuclei through nuclear activity, be it at the time of the big bang (primordial nucleosynthesis, responsible for the light elements such as hydrogen and helium), at the centre of the great red stars (where heavier elements than helium and lighter than iron are produced), or in the supernovas (the explosive deaths of stars that have consumed their fuel, where the remaining elements that are heavier than iron are forged).

Ontological: having to do with the essence, with the deep identity, with the nature of a being, such as essential care with relation to the human being.

Panentheism: literally means everything is in God and God in everything; it is a doctrine that affirms the mutual presence of creatures in God and of God in creatures. Panentheism presupposes the difference between creature and God and is distinct from pantheism, which negates this difference and affirms that everything is God.

Paradigm: a system of principles, ideas and values that are shared by a community and that serves as a reference and guidance. A paradigm shift occurs when a new way of seeing reality emerges, as is happening in modern times.

Pathos: the capacity to feel or a profound feeling; it is the root of words such as 'sympathy', 'pathetic' and 'patient'.

Primordial elements: chemical elements that were produced at the time of the big bang and during the first three minutes of the universe. These were mainly hydrogen, which composed about three-quarters of all the mass in the universe, helium, which composed about one-quarter, and a few traces of deuterium and lithium.

Quantum physics: theory developed at the beginning of the twentieth century that describes the properties of matter and of energies at the subatomic level. According to this theory, matter and light can be considered simultaneously as particle and wave. They can be described only in terms of probability. The particle of light is called a quantum of energy, and thus the name of the theory (see also *Quantum vacuum* and *Complementarity principle*).

Quantum vacuum: space full of virtual particles and antiparticles that appear and disappear in a fraction of a second. Everything comes from and returns to the quantum vacuum because it is the original fountain of everything that exists and that may exist in the order of things that we know.

Self-organization: the spontaneous organization of matter and of the original energies that give origin to live beings, and which is also called *autopoiesis*.

Strong nuclear force: the force that connects quarks (the most elemental of particles) so that protons and neutrons can be formed, and that connects protons and neutrons to form atomic nuclei. It does not act on photons and electrons. It is the most powerful force of nature.

Sustainability: it is said that a society or a process of development has sustainability when it is able to provide for all needs without compromising natural resources, and without damaging the rights that future generations have of seeing their needs fulfilled and of inheriting a planet that is in order and with its ecosystems preserved.

Symbiosis: the association between different living species for mutual benefit; and by extension of this, the association between living beings, social systems and machines, a development that is concretely taking place in modern societies.

Synergy: the interaction of all energies present in an ecosystem aiming at the maintenance of the ecosystem and of each being in this system.

Tao: the central concept of Taoism, which is difficult to explain. It can be understood as the path of the universe, of things and of people, or as the primordial energy that enables the path to be followed, the energy that is in everything and that guides everything. When the Tao is interiorized by a person it stands for transfiguration and the union with the Whole and with all.

Taoism: religion and philosophy with its origins in China (fourth century BC) and based on *Tao* as explained above. Its main representatives are Lao-tse and Chuang-tsu.

Thermodynamics: a branch of physics and chemistry that studies heat and its changes. There are two basic laws. The first affirms that heat is energy and that it is always constant in the universe. The second affirms that heat (energy) always suffers from a non-recoverable dissipation. This is called entropy. A closed system has the tendency to use up all its energy and to stabilize itself in thermic death. An open system experiences synthropy; that is, the capacity to reduce the effects of entropy and to create new orders that are less energy-hungry.

Upanishad: Sanskrit word that designates the holy texts of the Hindus, which are considered to be a divine revelation. These texts date from the end of the Vedic period (700–300 BC). They interpret the Vedas and insist on the necessity of freeing oneself from the cycle of births through knowledge of the illusion of reality.

Weak nuclear force: it is responsible for the disintegration of atoms and for radioactivity. It acts only at the atomic level.

Zen Buddhism: a branch of Buddhism that was diffused in Japan in the thirteenth century and which focuses on the value of meditation (*zen*) without images, on loving nature and on the practice of manual work that helps develop self-control and self-knowledge.

Notes and further reading

Foreword

Note

1 NB. All words with the symbol * are found in the Glossary.

Chapter 1

Note

1 Translation note: the word Boff uses here in Portuguese is *religação*, which is equivalent to the English word 'reconnection', and I have opted for a direct translation. It is important to note that when Boff uses this Portuguese word with a hyphen he usually has in mind a play on words with the Portuguese word *re-ligiao* or the English word 'religion', since the origin of these words in Portuguese is the Latin verb *re-ligare* or 'to reconnect' in English. I have drawn the reader's attention to this fact here because the direct translation 're-connection' with a hyphen will reoccur in different parts of the text.

Further Reading

Antunes, C., *Uma Aldeia em perigo. Os grandes problemas geográficos do século XX*, Petrópolis: Vozes, 1986.

Araújo de Oliveira, M., *Ética e práxis histórica*, São Paulo: Ática, 1995.

Arrighi, G., *A Ilusão do desenvolvimento*, Petrópolis: Vozes, 1997.

——, *The Long Twentieth Century: Money, Power, and the Origins of Our Times*, London: Verso, 1994.

Arruda, M., *Globalization and Civil Society: Rethinking Cooperativism in the Context of Active Citizenship*, Rio de Janeiro: PACS, 1996.

Assmann, H., *Metáforas novas para reencantar a educação*, Piracicaba: Editora UNIMEP, 1996.

——, *Reencantar a educação. Rumo à sociedade aprendente*, Petrópolis: Vozes, 1998.

Barrère, M., *Terre, patrimoine commun*, Paris: La Découverte, 1992.

Berry, T., *The Dream of the Earth*, San Francisco: Sierra Club Books, 1990.

Boff, L., *Cry of the Earth, Cry of the Poor*, Maryknoll, NY: Orbis Books, 1997.

——, *Global Civilization: Challenges to Society and Christianity*, London and Oakville: Equinox, 2005.

——, *O despertar da águia. O dia-bólico e o sim-bólico na construção da realidade*, Petrópolis: Vozes, 1998.

Boff, L., and Frei Betto, *Mística e Espiritualidade*, Rio de Janeiro: Rocco, 1995.

Capra, F., *The Web of Life: A New Scientific Understanding of Living Systems*, New York: Anchor, 1997.

Demo, P., *Conhecimento moderno. Sobre ética e intervenção do conhecimento*, Petrópolis: Vozes, 1994.

Featherstone, M., *Global Culture: Nationalism, Globalization and Modernity*, London: Sage, 1990.

Ferguson, M., *The Aquarian Conspiracy: Personal and Social Transformations in the 1980s*, Los Angeles: Tarcher, 1979.

Ferry, L., *The New Ecological Order*, Chicago: Chicago University Press, 1995.

Fiori, J. L., *Os Moedeiros falsos*, Petrópolis: Vozes, 1997.

Freud, S., *Civilization and its Discontents*, New York: W. W. Norton, 1989.

Guiton, J., *Deus e a ciência*, Rio de Janeiro: Nova Fronteira, 1992.

Heisenberg, W., *A parte e o todo*, Rio de Janeiro: Contraponto, 1996.

Hirst, P., and Thompson, G., *Globalization in Question: The International Economy and the Possibilities of Governance*, Cambridge: Polity Press, 1999.

Ianni, O., *A era do globalismo*, Rio de Janeiro: Civilização Brasileira, 1996.

Johnson, G., *Fire in the Mind: Science, Faith and the Search for Order*, Westminster, MD: Knopf, 1995.

Ladrière, J., *Les enjeux de la rationalité. Le défi de la science e de la technologie aux cultures*, Paris: Aubier, 1977.

Latouche, S., *L'occidentalisation du monde: Essai sur la signification, la portée et les limites de l'uniformisation planétaire*, Paris: Editions La Découverte, 2005.

Lemkow, A. F., *The Wholeness Principle: Dynamics of Unity Within Science, Religion and Society*, Wheaton, IL: Theosophical Publishing House, 1990.

Lovelock, J., *The Ages of Gaia*, Oxford: Oxford University Press, 1988.

Matellard, A., *Communicação-mundo*, Petrópolis: Vozes, 1994.

May, P. H., and Motta, R. S., *Valorando a natureza. Análise econômica para o desenvolvimento sustentável*, São Paulo: Campus, 1994.

McKibben, B., *The End of Nature*, Bloomsbury Publishing, 2004.

Meslin, M., *A experiência humana do divino*, Petrópolis: Vozes, 1992.

Müller, R., *The Birth of a Global Civilization*, Anacortes, WA: World Happiness and Cooperation, 1992.

Ramonet, I., *Geopolitics of Chaos*, New York: Algora Publishing, 1998.

Sagan, C., *The Demon-Haunted World: Science as a Candle in the Dark*, New York: Ballantine Books, 1997.

———, *Pale Blue Dot: A Vision of the Human Future in Space*, New York: Random House, 1994.

Schwarz, W., and Schwarz, D., *Ecologia: alternativa de futuro*, São Paulo: Paz e Terra, 1990.

Serres, M., *The Natural Contract*, Ann Arbor: University of Michigan Press, 1995.

Sklair, L., *Sociology of the Global System*, London: Prentice-Hall, 1990.

Vieira, L., *Cidadania e globalização*, Rio de Janeiro: Nova Fronteira, 1991.

Vos, H. V., *Utopia cristã e lógica econômica*, Petrópolis: Vozes, 1997.

Ward, P., *The End of Evolution: On Mass Extinctions and the Preservation of Biodiversity*, Westminster, MD: Bantam Dell Pub Group, 1994.

Chapter 2

Notes

1 Martin Heidegger, *Being and Time*, trans. John Macquarrie and Edward Robinson, Oxford: Blackwell, 2004, § 193, p. 238.

2 Heidegger, *Being and Time*, § 196, p. 240.

Further Reading

Araújo de Oliveira, M., *Ética e racionalidade moderna*, São Paulo: Loyola, 1993.

Arendt, H., *The Human Condition*, Chicago: University of Chicago Press, 1999.

Benhabib, S., and Cornell, D. (eds.), *Feminism as Critique: On the Politics of Gender*, Minneapolis: University of Minnesota Press, 1987.

Boff, L., *The Maternal Face of God*, San Francisco: HarperCollins, 1989.

——, *O destino do homen e do mundo*, Petrópolis: Vozes, 1996.

Bolen, J. S., *Goddesses in Everywoman: A New Psychology of Women*, New York: Harper Perennial, 1985.

Buytendijk, J. F. F., *La femme, ses modes d'être, de paraître et d'exister*, Paris: Desclée de Brower, 1987.

Campbell, J., *As transformacoes do mito através do tempo*, São Paulo: Cultrix, 1992.

——, *Todos os nomes da Deusa*, Rio de Janeiro: Rosa dos Tempos, 1997.

Capra, F., *The Tao of Physics*, London: Flamingo, 1992.

Carotenuto, A., *Eros and Pathos: The Far Side of Passion*, Toronto: Inner City Books, 1990.

Cardoso, S., *et al.*, *Os sentidos da paixão*, São Paulo: Companhia das Letras, 1998.

Cassirer, E., *Antropologia filosófica*, São Paulo: Mestre Jou, 1972.

——, *An Essay on Man*, New Haven: Yale University Press, 1962.

Chardin, P. T., *The Phenomenon of Man*, London: Harper Perennial, 1976.

Charon, J. E., *Unknown Spirit*, London: Coventure Ltd, 1983.

Coveny, P., and Highfield, R., *The Arrow of Time*, New York: Fawcett Columbine, 1990.

Davies, P., *The Cosmic Blueprint: New Discoveries in Nature's Creative Ability to Order the Universe*, New York: Touchstone Books, 1989.

Dirani, Z. C., *O despertar da mulher é o despertar do homem*, Rio de Janeiro: Espaço e Tempo, 1986.

Duve, C., *Vital Dust: Life as a Cosmic Imperative*, New York: Basic Books, 1994.

Edinger, E. F., *The Christian Archetype: A Jungian Commentary on the Life of Christ*, Toronto: Inner City Books, 1987.

Faros, F., *A natureza de eros*, São Paulo: Paulus, 1998.

Ferris, T., *O céu da mente. A inteligência humana num contexto cósmico*, São Paulo: Campus, 1993.

Fox, M., *Coming of the Cosmic Christ: The Healing of Mother Earth and the Birth of a Global Renaissance*, San Francisco: Harper & Row, 1988.

Galbraith, J. K., *The Good Society: The Humane Agenda*, Boston: Houghton Mifflin, 1996.

Giddens, A., *Transformation of Intimacy: Sex, Love, and Eroticism in Modern Societies*, Stanford, CA: Stanford University Press, 1993.

Gleick, J., *Chaos: Making a New Science*, New Jersey: E. Rutherford, 1988.

Gleiser, M., *The Dancing Universe: From Creation Myths to the Big Bang*, New York: E. P. Dutton, 1997.

Hawley, J., *Reawakening the Spirit in Work: The Power of Dharmic Management*, San Francisco: Berret-Koehler Publishers, 1993.

Heidegger, M., *Being and Time*, trans. John Macquarrie and Edward Robinson, Oxford: Blackwell, 2004.

Hollis, J., *Tracking the Gods: The Place of Myth in Modern Life*, Toronto: Inner City Books, 1995.

Imbasciatti, A., *Affetto e rappresentazione*, Milan: Franco Angeli, 1991.

Johnson, G., *Fire in the Mind: Science, Faith and the Search for Order*, Westminster, MD: Knopf, 1995.

Leonard, G., *Education and Ecstasy*, New York: Delacorte Press, 1968.

Maturana, H., and Varela, F., *The Tree of Knowledge: The Biological Roots of Human Understanding*, Boston: Shambhala, 1987.

Margulis, S., and Sagan, D., *Microcosmos*, New York: Simon & Schuster, 1991.

May, R., *The Courage to Create*, New York: W. W. Norton, 1994.

——, *Love and Will*, New York: W. W. Norton, 1969.

Morin, E., *O problema epistemológico da complexidade*, Lisboa: Publicações Europa-América, 1985.

Neumann, E., *The Origins and History of Consciousness*, Princeton, NJ: Princeton University Press, 1995.

Novello, M., *O círculo do tempo*, Rio de Janeiro: Campus, 1997.

Oliveira, A. B., *A unidade perdida homem-universo. Uma visão aberta da physis no fim do milenio*, Rio de Janeiro: Espaço e Tempo, 1989.

Paulon, E., *John Bowlby num encontro de Ciência e Ternura*, Niterói: Arte e Cultura, 1991.

Pearson, C. S., *The Hero Within*, San Francisco: HarperSanFrancisco, 1989.

Pegoraro, O., *Ética é justiça*, Petrópolis: Vozes, 1995.

Restrepo, L. C., *O direito à ternura*, Petrópolis: Vozes, 1998.

Sagan, C., *Pale Blue Dot: A Vision of the Human Future in Space*, New York: Random House, 1994.

Schnittman, D. F. (ed.), *Novos paradigmas, cultura e subjectividade*, Porto Alegre: Artes Médicas, 1996.

Smart, J. J. C., *Our Place in the Universe: A Metaphysical Discussion*, Oxford: Blackwell, 1989.

Todorov, T., *The Morals of History*, Minneapolis: University of Minnesota Press, 1995.

Unger, N. M., *O encantamento humano*, São Paulo, Loyola, 1991.

Weber, R., *Dialogues with Scientists and Sages*, New York: Routledge & Kegan Paul, 1986.

Zohar, D., *The Quantum Self*, New York: Harper Perennial, 1991.

Chapter 3
Notes

1 The Latin text by Higgins is available in Martin Heidegger's *Being and Time*, trans. John Macquarrie and Edward Robinson, Oxford: Blackwell, § 197–198, p. 242.

2 The English translation of the text by Higgins is also available in Martin Heidegger's *Being and Time*, § 198, p. 242.

Chapter 4
Note

1 The most secure data about Gaius Julius Hyginus is found in *Paulys Realencyclopediae der Classischen Altertumswissenschaft*, vol. 19, Stuttgart: 1918, columns 628–51.

Chapter 5
Notes

1 Translation note: the *Oxford English Dictionary* defines 'factoid' as 'an item of unreliable information that is repeated so often that it becomes accepted as fact'.

2 Translation note: Dom Hélder Câmara became Archbishop of Olinda and Recife in 1964, and in 1985 he reached the age of retirement and became Emeritus Archbishop. While Bishop of Rio de Janeiro he was baptized as the 'Bishop of the Slums'. He was extremely involved in defending the rights of the poor and founded a number of charities and organizations to help the Brazilian poor. He was also very critical of the military dictatorship that was established in Brazil in 1964, the year in which he

became Archbishop of Olinda and Recife. He died at the age of 90 on 27 August 1999.

3 Translation note: Tupi is the name of one of the main ethnic groups that are indigenous to the Brazilian territory (although they are also present in other South American countries). The Tupi, together with the Guarani, form the Tupi–Guarani nation of indigenous people. They were largely exterminated, enslaved or assimilated by the Portuguese conquerors. It is thought that in 1500, the official year of the discovery of Brazil, up to 10 million indigenous Indians lived in Brazil; today, however, this figure is estimated to be between 100,000 and 190,000 including those who live in urban centres. The decrease in numbers is the outcome of the Portuguese conquest and of the spread of diseases that were unknown in the Americas by European colonists. Despite this, many Tupi–Guarani words have made their way into Brazilian Portuguese, especially as the names of places, plants, fruits and animals.

4 Translation note: the correct English translation for the word *mandioca* is 'manioc'. I have opted to keep the original Brazilian Portuguese or Tupi–Guarani word here, since it reads well within the context of the Tupi myth. The origin of this word is the composite of two Tupi words: *Mandi* and *oca*. Mandi is the name of the girl who was buried in her own communal hut, which is *oca* in Tupi. However, the composite of these two words assumes the meaning 'the body of Mandi', as Boff points out later in the text.

5 Translation note: *Rei Momo* is the king of the Brazilian carnival. The title has its origins in Greek mythology where Momo was the son of Dream and of Night (Hypnos and Nix); he was the god of jokes, mockery, sarcasm, and irreverence. The coronation of a King Momo on Earth is an ancient Roman tradition where, during certain festivals, the most beautiful soldier was crowned as a joyful king who could do everything, from eating to playing, and no one could stop him. In Brazil the tradition was established in 1933 when a journalist presented a puppet to people playing in the carnival and suggested that it should lead the parade.

6 Translation note: I understand that by writing 'the flight of the eagle' and 'the pecking of the chicken', Boff is alluding to the fable of the eagle and the chicken, and to his book *A Águia e a Galinha* (The

Eagle and the Chicken), Petropólis: Vozes, 1997 (not available in English).

Further Reading

Baldus, H., *Lendas dos índios brasileiros*, São Paulo: Brasiliense, 1946.

Bolen, J. S., *Goddesses in Everywoman: A New Psychology of Women*, New York: Harper Perennial, 1985.

Brandão, J. de Souza, *Dicionário mítico-etimológico da mitologia grega*, Petrópolis: Vozes, 1991.

——, *Dicionário mítico-etimológico da mitologia e da religião romano*, Petrópolis e Brasília: Vozes e UnB Editora, 1993.

——, *Mitologia grega I–III*, Petrópolis: Vozes, 1995.

Brunel, P. (ed.), *Companion to Literary Myths, Heroes and Archetypes*, London: Routledge, 1996.

Campbell, J., *The Hero with a Thousand Faces*, Princeton, NJ: Princeton University Press, 1973.

Cassirer, E., *Language and Myth*, New York: Dover Publications, 1953.

Costa e Silva, A., *Lendas do índio brasileiro*, Belem e Rio de Janeiro: Biblioteca A. Viana, 1957.

Chevaier, J., and Gheerbrant, A., *A Dictionary of Symbols*, Oxford: Blackwell, 1994.

Hollis, J., *Tracking the Gods: The Place of Myth in Modern Life*, Toronto: Inner City Books, 1995.

Jaeger, W., *Paideia: The Ideals of Greek Culture*, New York and Oxford: Oxford University Press, 1967.

Kury, M. G., *Dicionário de mitologia grega e romana*, Rio de Janeiro: Zahar, 1997.

Lesky, A., *Greek Tragedy*, London: E. Benn, 1965.

Paris, G., *Pagan Meditations: The Worlds of Aphrodite, Artemis, and Hestia*, Dallas: Spring Publications, 1986.

Patai, R., *Myth and Modern Man*, Englewood Cliffs, NJ: Prentice-Hall, 1972.

Pearson, C. S., *The Hero Within*, San Francisco: HarperSanFrancisco, 1989.

Woolger, J. B., and Woolger, R. J., *The Goddess Within: A Guide to the Eternal Myths that Shape Women's Lives*, New York: Fawcett Columbine, 1987.

Chapter 6

Notes

1 Translation note: see *Nucleosynthesis* and *Primordial elements* entries in the Glossary.
2 Translation note: see *Noosphere* entry in the Glossary.
3 The *Pacha Mama* or the *Mama Pacha*, who is worshipped in Inca mythology. She was a dragon fertility goddess who presided over agriculture, and she is today identified with the Virgin Mary in some regions of Peru.
4 Nanã, an *orixá* or deity from the pantheon of African religions, such as Umbanda and Camdomblé, which are widely present in Brazil. These religions were brought over by slaves, and they resisted all attempts made by the Portuguese to suppress them. Nanã is the first Great Mother in the mythology of these religions.
5 Translation note: I understand that Boff refers here to deities such as the Indian goddess Kali (Great Black Mother) and the Chinese goddess Si-wang-mu (Mother Queen goddess), but please note that there are many other examples of deities that fit these two terms.

Further Reading

Atlan, H., *Entre le Cristal e la Fumée*, Paris: Seuil, 1986.
Barrow, J. D., *Theories of Everything*, New York: Ballantine, 1991.
Boff, L., *Cry of the Earth, Cry of the Poor*, Maryknoll, NY: Orbis Books, 1997.
Bohm, D., *Science, Order and Creativity*, New York: Bantam Books, 1987.
Bohr, N., *Atomic Physics and Human Knowledge*, New York: Interscience, 1963.
Capra, F., *The Turning Point*, New York: Bantam, 1983.
——, *The Web of Life: A New Scientific Understanding of Living Systems*, New York: Anchor, 1997.
Charon, J. E., *Unknown Spirit*, London: Coventure Ltd, 1983.
Duve, C., *Vital Dust: Life as a Cosmic Imperative*, New York: Basic Books, 1994.
Davies, P., *God and the New Physics*, New York: Simon & Schuster, 1983.
Dawkins, R., *River out of Eden: A Darwinian View of Life*, New York: HarperCollins, 1995.
Dumas, F. D., *L'oeuf cosmique: Le symbolisme de la genèse universelle*, St Jean de Braye, France: Editions Dangles, 1979.

Ehrlich, P. R., *The Machinery of Nature*, New York: Simon & Schuster, 1986.

Einstein, A., *The World as I See It*, New York: Philosophical Library, 1949.

Faros, F., *A natureza de eros*, São Paulo: Paulus, 1998.

Ferris, T., *Coming of Age in the Milky Way*, New York: HarperCollins, 2003.

Frei Betto, *A obra do artista. Uma visão holística do Universo*, São Paulo: Ática, 1995.

Freire-Maia, N., *Criação e evolução: Deus, o acaso e a necessidade*, Petrópolis: Vozes, 1986.

Gleick, J., *Chaos: Making a New Science*, New Jersey: E. Rutherford, 1988.

Gleiser, M., *The Dancing Universe: From Creation Myths to the Big Bang*, New York: E. P. Dutton, 1997.

Goswani, A., *The Self-Aware Universe*, New York: Penguin Putnam, 1995.

Gribbin, J., *In the Beginning: After Cobe and Before the Big Bang*, Boston: Little, Brown, 1993.

Guth, A. H., *The Inflationary Universe*, New York: Perseus Books, 1998.

Harada, H., 'Fenomenologia do Corpo', in *Revista de Cultura Vozes*, No 65, 1971, pp. 21–28.

Hawking, S., *A Brief History of Time*, New York: Bantam Books, 1988.

Heisenberg, W., *A parte e o todo*, Rio de Janeiro: Contraponto, 1996.

Hollis, J., *Tracking the Gods: The Place of Myth in Modern Life*, Toronto: Inner City Books, 1995.

Jacob, F., *The Logic of Life*, Princeton, NJ: Princeton University Press, 1973.

Johnson, G., *Fire in the Mind: Science, Faith and the Search for Order*, Westminster, MD: Knopf, 1995.

Laborit, H., *Dieu ne joue pas aux dés*, Paris: Grasset, 1987.

Lewin, R., *Complexity: Life at the Edge of Chaos*, New York: Macmillan, 1992.

Lindfield, M., *The Dance of Change. An Eco-Spiritual Approach to Transformation*, London: Arkana, 1986.

Longair, M., *The Origins of Our Universe*, Cambridge: Cambridge University Press, 1990.

Lovelock, J., *Gaia: A New Look at Life on Earth*, Oxford: Oxford University Press, 2000.

Maturana, H., and Varela, F., *The Tree of Knowledge: The Biological Roots of Human Understanding*, Boston: Shambhala, 1992.

Monod, J., *Chance and Necessity*, New York: Knopf, 1971.

Mourão, R. R. F., *Buracos negros. Universo em colapso*, Petrópolis: Vozes, 1981.

——, *Ecologia cósmica. Uma visão cósmica da ecologia*, Rio de Janeiro: Francisco Alves, 1992.

——, *Nascimento, vida e morte das estrelas*, Petrópolis: Vozes, 1995.

Novello, M., *O círculo do tempo*, Rio de Janeiro: Campus, 1997.

Pessi-Pasternak, G., *Do caos à inteligência artificial*, São Paulo: UNESP, 1992.

Reeves, H., et al., *A mais bela história do mundo. Os segredos de nossas origens*, Petrópolis: Vozes, 1998.

Salam, A., *Unification of Fundamental Forces*, Cambridge: Cambridge University Press, 2005.

Sagan, C., *Billions and Billions: Thoughts of Life and Death at the Brink of the Millennium*, New York: Ballantine Books, 1997.

——, *Cosmos*, New York: Ballantine Books, 1985.

——, *Pale Blue Dot: A Vision of the Human Future in Space*, New York: Random House, 1994.

Sahtouris, E., *Earth Dance: Living Systems in Evolution*, Santa Cruz, CA: Rat Haus Reality Press, 1996.

Steiger, A., *Comprende l'histoire de la vie*, Lyon: Chronique sociale, 1995.

Ward, P., *The End of Evolution: On Mass Extinctions and the Preservation of Biodiversity*, Westminster, MD: Bantam Dell Pub Group, 1994.

Weil, P., *A consciência cósmica*, Petrópolis: Vozes, 1989.

Weinberg, S., *The First Three Minutes: A Modern View of the Origin of the Universe*, New York: Basic Books, 1988.

Wilson, E. O., and Peter, F. (eds.), *Biodiversity*, Washington, DC: National Academy Press, 1988.

Chapter 7

Notes

1 Heidegger, M., *Being and Time*, trans. John Macquarrie and Edward Robinson, Oxford: Blackwell, 2004, § 199, p. 243.

2 Heidegger, *Being and Time*, § 200, p. 244.

3 For the philology of the word 'care' it is advisable to consult the following sources: *Thesaurus Linguae Latinae*, vol. 4, Leipzig,

1909, col. 1451–76; *Paulys Realencyclopaedia der Classischen Altertumswissenschaft*, vol. 8, Stuttgart, 1901, col. 1773; Ernout, A., and Meillet, A., *Dictionnaire Ethymologique de la Langue Latine*, Paris, 1939, pp. 245–6; 'Cuidado', Caldas Aulete, *Dicionário Contemporâneo da Língua Portuguesa*, Rio de Janeiro: Edições Delta, 1985; Antenor Nascentes, *Dicionário Etimológico Resumido*, Rio de Janeiro: Instituto Nacional do Livro, 1966; Antônio Geraldo da Cunha, *Dicionário Etimológico Nova Fronteira da Língua Portuguesa*, Rio de Janeiro: Nova Fronteira, 1991.

4 Translation note: Father Antônio Vieira was born in Lisbon in 1608 and as a boy emigrated with his parents to Brazil where he died in the state of Bahia in 1697. He was a Jesuit priest and is considered one of the main writers of Brazilian and Portuguese baroque prose. He wrote a number of sermons, of which the *Sermão pelo bom sucesso das armas de Portugal contra as de Holanda* is of particular interest for the Portuguese; in this he asks God to put a stop to the victories of the Dutch Protestant heretic armies that are fighting Portugal. To the Brazilian the *Sermão da Primeira Dominga da Quaresma* and the *Sermão XIV do Rosário* are of particular interest. In the former, Vieira tries to persuade colonists to free the enslaved indigenous Indians and compares these to the Jews enslaved by the pharaoh; in the latter, he compares the sufferings of black slaves to the sufferings of Christ.

5 Antoine de Saint-Exupéry, *The Little Prince*, trans. Katherine Woods, London: William Heinemann, 1944, p. 68.

6 Daniel Goleman, *Intelligência Emocional*, Rio de Janeiro: Objectiva, 1995. The quote is available in the 'Introduction' to the Brazilian edition, p. 3; *Emotional Intelligence: Why It Can Matter More than IQ*, New York: Bantam, 1994.

Further Reading

Boff, L., *O destino do homem e do mundo*, Petrópolis: Vozes, 1976.

——, *O princípio-Terra. Volta à pátria comum*. São Paulo: Ática, 1995.

——, *The Maternal Face of God: The Feminine and its Religious Expressions*, London: Collins, 1979.

Buytendijk, J. F. F., *La femme, ses modes d'être, de paraître et d'exister*, Paris: Desclée de Brower, 1967.

Campos Paes, E., *Quem cuida do cuidador*, Petrópolis: Vozes, 2005.

Capra, F., *The Tao of Physics*, London: Flamingo, 1992.

Cardoso, S., *et al.*, *Os sentidos da paixão*, São Paulo: Companhia das Letras, 1998.

Carotenuto, A., *Eros and Pathos: The Far Side of Passion*, Toronto: Inner City Books, 1990.

Cavalieri, P., and Singer, P. (eds.), *El proyeto 'Gran Sime' – La igualdad más allá de la humanidad*, Madrid: Trotta, 1998.

Chardin, P. T., *The Phenomenon of Man*, London: Harper Perennial, 1976.

Crespo, J., *História do corpo*, Rio de Janeiro: Bertrand, 1990.

Demo, P., *Conhecimento moderno. Sobre ética e intervenção do conhecimento*, Petrópolis: Vozes, 1998.

Duve, C., *Vital Dust: Life as a Cosmic Imperative*, New York: Basic Books, 1994.

Gadamer, H. G., *Reason in the Age of Science*, Cambridge, MA: MIT Press, 1963.

Giddens, A., *Transformation of Intimacy: Sex, Love, and Eroticism in Modern Societies*, Stanford, CA: Stanford University Press, 1993.

Goleman, D., *Emotional Intelligence: Why It Can Matter More than IQ*, New York: Bantam, 1994.

Gutiérrez, R., *O feminismo é um humanismo*, Rio de Janeiro: Nobel-Antares, 1985.

Habermas, J., *Knowledge and Human Interest*, Cambridge: Polity Press, 1987.

Heidegger, M., *Being and Time*, trans. John Macquarrie and Edward Robinson, Oxford: Blackwell, 2004.

Imbasciatti, A., *Affetto e rappresentazione*, Milan: Franco Angeli, 1991.

Leonard, G., *Education and Ecstasy*, New York: Delacorte Press, 1968.

Matos, L., *Corpo e mente*, Petrópolis: Vozes, 1994.

Maturana, H., and Varela, F., *A ontologia da realidade*, Belo Horizonte: Editora UFMG, 1997.

——, *Autopoiesis and Cognition: The Realization of the Living*, New York: Springer, 2001.

——, *The Tree of Knowledge: The Biological Roots of Human Understanding*, Boston: Shambhala, 1987.

May, R., *The Courage to Create*, New York: W. W. Norton, 1994.

——, *Love and Will*, New York: W. W. Norton, 1969.

Miranda, R. L., *Além da inteligência emocional*, Rio de Janeiro: Campus, 1998.

Muraro, R. M., *A mulher no terceiro milênio*, Rio de Janeiro: Rosa dos Tempos, 1992.

Neumann, E., *The Origins and History of Consciousness*, Princeton, NJ: Princeton University Press, 1995.

Noddings, N., *Caring: A Feminine Approach to Ethics and Moral Education*, Berkeley: University of California Press, 1984.

——, 'Two concepts of caring', in *Philosophy of Education* 1999, Illinois: Urbana, 2000.

Novello, M., *O círculo do tempo*, Rio de Janeiro: Campus, 1997.

Oliveira, A. B., *A unidade perdida homem-universo. Uma visão aberta da physis no fim do milenio*, Rio de Janeiro: Espaço e Tempo, 1989.

Paris, G., *Pagan Meditations: The Worlds of Aphrodite, Artemis, and Hestia*, Dallas: Spring Publications, 1986.

Paulon, E., *John Bowlby num encontro de Ciência e Ternura*, Niterói: Arte e Cultura, 1991.

Restrepo, L. C., *O direito à ternura*, Petrópolis: Vozes, 1998.

Roselló, F. T., *Antropología del cuidar*, Institut Borja de bioética, Madrid: Fundación Mapfre Medicina, 1998.

Rosnay, J. L., *Symbiotic Man*, New York: McGraw-Hill, 2000.

Sagan, C., *Pale Blue Dot: A Vision of the Human Future in Space*, New York: Random House, 1994.

Sjöö, M., and Mor, B., *The Great Cosmic Mother: Rediscovering the Religion of the Earth*, San Francisco: Harper, 1991.

Smart, J. J. C., *Our Place in the Universe: A Metaphysical Discussion*, Oxford: Blackwell, 1989.

Spindeldreier, Frei A., 'Feminilidade', in *Revista Grande Sinal*, No 40, 1970, pp. 83–92.

Susin, L. C., *O homem messiânico. Uma introdução ao pensamento de Emanuel Lévinas*, Petrópolis: Vozes, 1984.

Touraine, A., *Critique de la Modernité*, Paris: Fayard, 1992.

Unger, N. M., *O encantamento humano*, São Paulo, Loyola, 1991.

Vattimo, G., *The End of Modernity. Nihilism and Hermeneutics in Postmodern Culture*, Baltimore, MD: Johns Hopkins University Press, 1991.

Waldow, V. R., *Cuidado humano: o resgate necessário*, Porto Alegre: Sagra-Luzatto, 1998.

Woolger, J. B., and Woolger, R. J., *The Goddess Within: A Guide to the Eternal Myths that Shape Women's Lives*, New York: Fawcett Columbine, 1987.

Chapter 8

Notes

1 Translated directly from the Portuguese. Humberto Maturana and Sima Nisis de Rezepka, *Formação humana e capacitação*, Petrópolis: Vozes, 2000, p. 75.

2 Luis Carlos Restrepo, *O direito à ternura*, Petrópolis: Vozes, 1998, p. 48.

3 Restrepo, *O direito à ternura*, p. 48.

4 Translation note: Capistrano de Abreu (1853–1927) is one of the first great Brazilian historians.

5 Antoine de Saint-Exupéry, *The Little Prince*, trans. Katherine Woods, London: William Heinemann, 1944, p. 68.

6 Translation note: I believe Boff has hyphenated the word 'cordiality' here to emphasize that the Latin stem *cor*, which means 'heart' in English, is present in this word.

7 This quote is available in Miguel-León Portilla, *Los antiguos mexicanos a través de sus crónicas y cantares*, Mexico: Fondo de Cultura Económica, 1961, p. 155.

8 Translation note: in the Portuguese original the word 'compassion' is hyphenated here, which implies a textual play between 'compassion' (*compaixão*) and 'with passion' (*com paixão*), and this also points out the derivation of the word 'compassion', which is 'with passion'.

9 Translation note: Matthew 5.45, RSV, reads: 'so that you may be sons of your Father who is in heaven; for he makes his sun rise on the evil and on the good, and sends rain on the just and on the unjust.' Luke 6.35, RSV, reads: 'But love your enemies, and do good, and lend, expecting nothing in return; and your reward will be great, and you will be sons of the Most High; for he is kind to the ungrateful and the selfish.'

10 Translation note: Matthew 25.36–41, RSV, reads: ' "I was naked and you clothed me, I was sick and you visited me, I was in prison and you came to me." Then the righteous will answer him, "Lord, when did we see thee hungry and feed thee, or thirsty and give thee drink? And when did we see thee a stranger and welcome thee, or naked and clothe thee? And when did we see thee sick or in prison and visit thee?" And the King will answer them, "Truly, I say to you, as you did it to one of the least of these my

brethren, you did it to me." Then he will say to those at his left hand, "Depart from me, you cursed, into the eternal fire prepared for the devil and his angels." '

Further Reading

Alberoni, F., *Falling in Love*, New York: Random House, 1982.

——, *L'erotismo*, Milano: Garzanti, 1986.

Appiah, K. A., *In My Father's House: Africa in the Philosophy of Culture*, New York and Oxford: Oxford University Press, 1992.

Arana, M. J., *Rescatar lo feminino para reanimar la Tierra*, Barcelona: Cristianismo e Justicia, 1998.

Assmann, H., *Metáforas novas para reencantar a educação*, Piracicaba: Editora UNIMEP, 1996.

——, *Reencantar a educação, Rumo à sociedade apreendente*. Petrópolis: Vozes, 1998.

Barletta, R., *El quinto mandamento*, Buenos Aires: Lohlé/Lumen, 1996.

Benhabib, S., and Cornell, D. (eds.), *Feminism as Critique: On the Politics of Gender*, Minneapolis: University of Minnesota Press, 1987.

Berry, T., *The Dream of the Earth*, San Francisco: Sierra Club Books, 1990.

Boff, L., *Brasa sob cinzas. Estórias do anticotidiano*, Rio de Janeiro: Record, 1997.

——, *Saint Francis: A Model of Human Liberation*, New York: Crossroad, 1982.

Carotenuto, A., *Eros and Pathos: The Far Side of Passion*, Toronto: Inner City Books, 1990.

Da Matta, R., *Ensaios de Antropologia estrutural*, Petrópolis: Vozes, 1977.

Demo, P., *Conhecimento moderno. Sobre ética e intervenção do conhecimento*, Petrópolis: Vozes, 1998.

Doczi, G., *The Power of Limits*, Boston, MA: Shambhala, 1981.

Fox, M., *A Spirituality Named Compassion*, Rochester, Vermont: Inner Traditions, 1999.

Giddens, A., *Transformation of Intimacy: Sex, Love, and Eroticism in Modern Societies*, Stanford, CA: Stanford University Press, 1993.

Harding, M. E., *Woman's Mysteries Ancient and Modern*, London: HarperCollins, 1976.

Hillman, J., *Insearch: Psychology and Religion*, Dallas: Spring Publications, 1987.

Holanda, S. B., 'O homem cordial', in *Raizes do Brasil*, Rio de Janeiro: José Olympio, 1989, pp. 101–112.

Imbasciatti, A., *Affetto e rappresentazione*, Milan: Franco Angeli, 1991.

Illich, I., *Tools for Conviviality*, London: Harper & Row, 1973.

Lenoble, R., *Esquisse d'une histoire de l'idée de nature*, Paris: Albin Michel, 1969.

León-Portilla, M., *Los antiguos mexicanos a través de sus crônicas y cantares*, Mexico: FCE, 1983.

Levy, P., *Collective Intelligence*, New York: Plenum, 1997.

Lewin, R., *Complexity: Life at the Edge of Chaos*, New York: Macmillan, 1992.

May, R., *Love and Will*, New York: W. W. Norton, 1969.

Paris, G., *Pagan Meditations: The Worlds of Aphrodite, Artemis, and Hestia*, Dallas: Spring Publications, 1986.

Prigogine, I., *The End of Certainty*, New York: Free Press, 1997.

Raymundo, J., *Auto-organizaçâo. Novas bases para o conhecimento humano?*, Rio de Janeiro: Ed. Idéia, 1993.

Restrepo, L. C., *O direito à ternura*, Petrópolis: Vozes, 1998.

Rose, K., *O corpo humano no tempo. Uma máchina com sentimentos, relações e transformações*, São Paulo: McGraw Hill, 1990.

Rouanet, S. P., *A razão cativa – As ilusões da consciência: de Platão a Freud*, São Paulo: Brasiliense, 1985.

Santos, B. S., *Pela mão de Alice. O social e o político na pós-modernidade*, São Paulo: Cortez, 1995.

Sheldrake, R., *The Rebirth of Nature*, New York: Bantam Books, 1991.

Smart, J. J. C., *Our Place in the Universe: A Metaphysical Discussion*, Oxford: Blackwell, 1989.

Susin, L. C., *O homem messiânico. Uma introdução ao pensamento de Emanuel Lévinas*, Petrópolis: Vozes, 1984.

Touraine, A., *Critique de la Modernité*, Paris: Fayard, 1992.

Velhelst, T., *O direito à diferença*, Petrópolis: Vozes, 1992.

Chapter 9

Notes

1 *Caring for the Earth: A Strategy for Sustainable Living*, IUCN, UNEP, WWF, 1991.

2 *Caring for the Earth*, p. 11.

3 Translation note: the word 'caboclo' is of Portuguese origin, and refers to a mixed-race person with one white European parent and one indigenous Brazilian Indian parent; the physical characteristics are copper-coloured skin and straight dark hair. *Mestiço*, which I have translated as 'mestizo', is the Portuguese term for someone who is descended from people with different ethnic backgrounds. Source: *Dicionário Aurélio*, 3a Edição Revista e Atualizada, Curitiba: Editora Positivo, 2004.

4 Donella H. Meadows, *et al.*, *The Limits to Growth*, New York: Universe Books, 1972.

5 'Declaration on the Rights to Development', Office of the High Commissioner for Human Rights, adopted by General Assembly resolution 41/128 of 4 December 1986. Available online on http://www.unhchr.ch/html/menu3/b/74.htm

6 Translation note: personalism is a philosophical movement that has its roots in the nineteenth century and that flourished in the twentieth century. It could be defined as the attempt to place persons and personal relations at the centre of theory and practice in various fields, such as philosophy, theology and politics. It could be said to be the middle way between collectivism and individualism. Major philosophers in this area are Romano Guardini, Enmanuel Levinas, Gabriel Marcel, Emmanuel Mournier, Martin Buber and Pope John Paul II, to name a few.

7 Translation note: I believe Boff has hyphenated the words 'pro-voke', 'e-voke' and 'con-voke' to draw attention to their etymology. It is probably easier for the native Portuguese speaker than it is for the English speaker to recognize the origin of these words since they are rooted in the Latin language. 'Provoke' from the Latin *provocare*, 'to challenge, to call forth', has its roots in the prefix 'pro-' meaning 'forth', and the verb *vocare*, 'to call'. 'Evoke' from the Latin *evocare*, 'to call out, to rouse, to summon', has its roots in the prefix 'ex-' meaning 'out' and the verb *vocare*, 'to call'. 'Convoke' from the Latin *convocare*, 'to call together', has its roots in the prefix 'com-' meaning 'together', and the verb *vocare*, 'to call'.

8 Translation note: as in note 7, 'pro-posal' is a noun derived from the prefix 'pro-' meaning 'forth' and the verb *ponere*, 'to put, to place'. 'Res-ponse' is a noun derived from the prefix 'res-' meaning 'back' and the verb *spondere*, 'to pledge'. 'Res-ponsi-bility' is

also a noun derived from the prefix 'res-' and the verb *spondere*, and it has assumed the meaning of 'being answerable to someone or to something or for one's own actions'.

9 Translation note: the definition of health is given in the Constitution of the World Health Organization, established in Geneva in 1946, and is available online on: http://w3.whosea. org/aboutsearo/pdf/const.pdf

10 Translation note: the quote is available in Porphyrius, *De Abstinentia II*, 19: 'In Epidaurus, at any rate, there was the inscription: "Pure must be he who enters the fragrant temple; purity means to think nothing but holy thoughts"', trans. Edelstein and Edelstein, *Asclepius*, Vol. I, T. 318, pp. 163–4; the passage is also quoted by Clement of Alexandria in *Stromata V*, i, 13 PG 9, cols 27–30, trans. Edelstein and Edelstein, *Asclepius*, Vol. I, T. 336, pp. 177–8. E. J. Edelstein, L. Edelstein and G. Ferngren, Introduction, *Asclepius: Collection and Interpretation of the Testimonies*, Johns Hopkins University Press, 1998.

11 Translation note: see *Noosphere* entry in the Glossary.

12 Translation note: I understand that Boff has hyphenated the words 'sym-bolic' and 'dia-bolic' to point out the etymology of the words. 'Symbolic' comes from the Greek 'sum-' or 'together' and *bolon*, 'to throw'; literally 'to throw together'. 'Diabolic' from the Greek dia- or 'across' and *bolon*, 'to throw'; literally 'to throw across'.

13 Translation note: the *Dicionário Aurélio da Língua Portuguesa* states that the Portuguese word *numinoso* comes from the Latin word *numen*, and this may be translated in English as 'divine will, or as a spiritual force associated with a natural object, place or phenomenon'. The *Dicionário Aurélio da Língua Portuguesa* also states that this Portuguese word is associated with the works of the German theologian and philosopher Rudolf Otto (1869–1927) and refers to the unique feeling associated with the religious experience, with the experience of the sacred, in which fascination, terror and overpowering are merged together. Indeed, the word 'numinous' is present in the English translation of Otto's *The Idea of the Holy*. There Otto states that the word comes from the Latin word *numen*, and he describes the 'numinous experience' as 'inexpressible and ineffable' (p. 5), and as possessing the attributes of awe (p. 13), overpowering (p. 19),

and fascination (p. 31). Sources: *Dicionário Aurélio da Língua Portuguesa*, 'Numinoso', Editora Positivo, 2004, p. 1417; Rudolf Otto, *The Idea of the Holy*, London: Oxford University Press, 1977.

14 Translation note: see *Panentheism* entry in the Glossary.

15 Translation note: 1 Corinthians 15.45, RSV: 'Thus it is written, "The first man Adam became a living being"; the last Adam became a life-giving spirit.'

Further Reading

Alves, R., *A construção social da enfermidade*, São Paulo: Cortez & Moraes, 1987.

Barrère, M., *Terre, patrimoine commun*, Paris: La Découverte, 1992.

Berry, T., *The Dream of the Earth*, San Francisco: Sierra Club Books, 1990.

Biase, F., *O homem holístico*, Petrópolis: Vozes, 1995.

Blofeld, J., *Bodhisattva of Compassion: The Mystical Tradition of Kuan Yin*, Boston: Shambhala, 1988.

Boff, L., *A nossa resurreição na morte*, Petrópolis: Vozes, 1996.

——, *A vida para além da morte*, Petrópolis: Vozes, 1997.

——, *Cry of the Earth, Cry of the Poor*, Maryknoll, NY: Orbis Books, 1997.

——, *Vida segundo of Espírito*, Petrópolis: Vozes, 1981.

Boff, L., and Frei Betto, *Mística e Espiritualidade*, Rio de Janeiro: Rocco, 1995.

Bonaventura, L., *Psicologia e mística*, Petrópolis: Vozes, 1978.

Campbell, J., *The Hero with a Thousand Faces*, Princeton, NJ: Princeton University Press, 1973.

Capra, F., *The Turning Point*, New York: Bantam, 1983.

Casaldáliga, P., and Virgil, J. M., *Espiritualidade e libertação*, Petrópolis: Vozes, 1993.

Crema, R., *Introdução à visão holística. Breve relato de viagem do velho ao novo paradigma*, São Paulo: Summus Editorial, 1988.

——, *Saúde e plenitude, um caminho para o ser*, São Paulo: Summus Editorial, 1995.

Ehrlich, P. R., *The Machinery of Nature*, New York: Simon & Schuster, 1986.

Einstein, A., *The World as I See It*, New York: Philosophical Library, 1949.

Frei Betto, *A obra do artista. Uma visão holística do Universo*, São Paulo: Ática, 1995.

Grupo TAO (Teologia e Assessoria Orgânica), *A mística do animador popular*, São Paulo: Ática, 1996.

Gutiérrez, G., *We Drink from Our Own Wells: The Spiritual Journey of a People*, Maryknoll, NY: Orbis Books, 1990.

Heisenberg, W., *A parte e o todo*, Rio de Janeiro: Contraponto, 1996.

Josaphat, C., *Contemplação e libertação*, São Paulo: Ática, 1995.

Leloup, J. Y., *Caminhos da realização. Dos medos do Eu ao mergulho no Ser*, Petrópolis: Vozes, 1996.

——, *Cuidar do Ser*, Petrópolis: Vozes, 1996.

——, *O corpo e seus símbolos. Uma antrologia essencial*, Petrópolis: Vozes, 1998.

Leloup, J. Y., Boff, L., *et al.*, *Espírito na saúde*, Petrópolis: Vozes, 1997.

Longair, M., *The Origins of Our Universe*, Cambridge: Cambridge University Press, 1990.

Lovelock, J., *The Ages of Gaia*, Oxford: Oxford University Press, 1988.

——, *Gaia: A New Look at Life on Earth*, Oxford: Oxford University Press, 2000.

Morin, E., *Ciência com consciência*, Rio de Janeiro: Francisco Alves, 1996.

Mourão, R. R. F., *Ecologia cósmica. Uma visão cósmica da ecologia*, Rio de Janeiro: Francisco Alves, 1992.

Müller, L., *O herói. Todos nascemos para ser heróis*, São Paulo: Cultrix, 1994.

Müller, R., *The Birth of a Global Civilization*, Anacortes, WA: World Happiness and Cooperation, 1992.

Prigogine, I., *A nova aliança. Metamorfose da ciência*, Brasília: Universidade de Brasília, 1990.

Rogers, C. R., *A pessoa como centro*, São Paulo: EDUSP, 1977.

Weil, P., *A morte da morte*, São Paulo: Gente, 1995.

——, *Antologia do êxtase*, São Paulo: Palas Athena, 1992.

Zohar, D., *The Quantum Self*, New York: Harper Perennial, 1991.

Chapter 10

Notes

1 Immanuel Kant, *Idea for a Universal History from a Cosmopolitan Point of View*, 1784. In *Kant's Principles of Politics*.

2 Translation note: Boff refers here to the hymn 'Come, Holy Spirit' or *'Veni, Sancte Spiritus'*, from the Roman Missal, trans. John Austin (1613–69).

Further Reading

Arendt, H., *The Origins of Totalitarianism*, New York: Harcourt, 1951.

Boff, L., 'Elementos de uma teologia da crise', in *A vida segundo o Espírito*, Petrópolis: Vozes, 1982, pp. 11–35.

——, *O despertar da águia. O dia-bólico e o sim-bólico na construção da realidade*, Petrópolis: Vozes, 1998.

Boudon, R., *The Unintended Consequences of Social Action*, London: Macmillan, 1982.

Brown, N. O., *Life against Death*, Middletown, CY: Wesleyan University Press, 1959.

França, M. I. (ed.), *Desejo, barbárie e cidadania*, Petrópolis: Vozes, 1995.

Gutiérrez, G., *On Job: God-Talk and the Suffering of the Innocent*, Maryknoll, NY: Orbis, 1987.

Horkheimer, M., *Eclipse of Reason*, New York: Continuum, 1974.

Krishnamurti, J., *Education and the Significance of Life*, New York: Harper & Row, 1953.

Leonard, G., *Education and Ecstasy*, New York: Delacorte Press, 1968.

Marcuse, H., *Eros and Civilization*, Boston: Beacon Press, 1955.

Restrepo, L. C., *O direito à ternura*, Petrópolis: Vozes, 1998.

Velho, G., *Desvio e divergência*, Rio de Janeiro: Zahar, 1983.

Chapter 11

Notes

1 Anne Sebba, *Mother Teresa: Beyond the Image*, London: Weidenfeld & Nicolson, 1997, p. 157.

2 Translation note: with the Napoleonic invasion of Portugal in 1807, the Portuguese royal family and court transferred themselves to Brazil. Soon after the Brazilian ports were declared open to foreign trade, and a number of changes took place, such as the creation of industries, libraries, banks and so on. Brazil and Portugal were also declared to be the United Kingdom of Portugal and Brazil. After independence from Portugal in 1822, when the Prince Regent Dom Pedro refused to return to Portugal, Brazil became the Empire of Brazil and Dom Pedro assumed the title of

Dom Pedro I. In 1889 the Republic of Brazil was established when the Brazilian Army became dissatisfied with the economic state of affairs of the country (in 1888 slaves were given their freedom by the Princess Regent Isabel and this brought serious consequences for the Brazilian economy), and the Brazilian imperial family was exiled to Europe (Portugal and then France). In 1920 the Law of Exile was revoked and the Brazilian imperial family was allowed back into the country. Because of family infighting there are two branches to the Brazilian imperial family: the branch of Petrópolis, which Boff refers to here, and the branch of Vassouras.

3 Translation note: in Portuguese F/S/G/L reads P/F/E/N for *Pai, Filho, Espirito Santo* and *Nossa Senhora*.

4 Translation note: Boff refers here to the UN Conference on Development and the Environment which was held 3–14 June 1992 in Rio de Janeiro.

5 Translated from the Portuguese. Leonardo Guelman, *Univvverrrsso Gentileza. A gênese de um mito contemporâneo*, Rio de Janeiro: Universidade Federal Fluminense/Pontuar, 1997, p. 231.

6 Translated from the Portuguese. Beatriz Bartoly, *Feng-shui e o desvelamento da morada humana. Um estudo sobre os conceitos de espaço e de natureza na filosofia chinesa*. Dissertation for Master's degree, Universidade Estadual do Rio de Janeiro, 1998, p. 204.

Further Reading

Alves, R., *Gandhi*, São Paulo: Brasiliense, 1983.

Alier, J. M., *Da economia ecológica ao ecologismo popular*, Blumenau: Editora FURB, 1998.

Bartoly, B., *Feng-shui e o desvelamento da morada humana. Um estudo sobre conceitos de espaço e de natureza na filosofia chinesa*, Dissertation for Master's degree, UERJ, 1998.

Boff, L., *Jesus Christ Liberator: A Critical Christology for Our Times*, New York: Orbis Books, 1978.

——, *Saint Francis: A Model of Human Liberation*, New York: Crossroad, 1982.

Debray, R., *Vie et mort de l'image*, Paris: Gallimard, 1995.

Eitel, E., *Feng Shui. The Science of Sacred Landscape in Old China*, Singapore: Synergetic Press, 1993.

Ellsberg, R., *Gandhi on Christianity*, New York: Orbis Books, 1991.

Englebert, O., *St Francis of Assisi. A Biography*, Ann Arbor, MI: Servant Books, 1979.

Fischer, L., *The Life of Mahatma Gandhi*, New York: HarperCollins, 1983.

Gandhi, M., *An Autobiography: The Story of My Experiments with Truth*, Boston: Beacon Press, 1962.

———, *The Words of Gandhi*, Attenborough, R. (ed.), New York: Newmarket Press, 1982.

Granet, M., *La pensée chinoise*, Paris: La Renaissance du Livre, 1934.

Guelman, L., *Univvversso Gentileza. A gênese de um mito contemporâneo*, Rio de Janeiro: Universidade Federal Fluminense/Pontuar, 1997.

Leclerc, E., *The Canticle of Creatures, Symbols of Union: An analysis of St. Francis of Assisi*, Chicago: Franciscan Herald Press, 1977.

Leloup, J. Y., and Boff, L., *Terapeutas do deserto*, Petrópolis: Vozes, 1997.

Leloup, J. Y., Boff, L., *et al.*, *Espírito na saúde*, Petrópolis: Vozes, 1997.

Lepargneur, H., *O despertar dos doentes*, Rio de Janeiro: Achiamé/ICAPS, 1986.

Remen, R. N., *Histórias que curam. Conversas sábias ao pé do fogo*, São Paulo: Ágora, 1998.

Rosnay, J. L., *Symbiotic Man*, New York: McGraw-Hill, 2000.

Sebba, A., *Mother Teresa: Beyond the Image*, New York: Doubleday, 1997.

Stilveman, M., *The Death March*, Rio de Janeiro: Imago, 2000.

Susin, L. C., *O homem messiânico. Uma introdução ao pensamento de Emanuel Lévinas*, Petrópolis: Vozes, 1984.

Index

Adam 33
Adler, Alfred 68
Alexander Polihistor 24–5
Alexander the Great 65
Asclepius (also Aesculapius) 106–8
Augustine, St 68

Bartoly, Beatriz 140
Bohr, Niels 68
Bonaventure, St 68, 122
Brother Antônio (Mendes de Ferreira): example of the way-of-being care 125–29
brothers Grimm 23
Buddha (also Siddhartha Gautama) 89–90, 121

Caesar, Gaius Julius 23–5
Câmara Cascudo, Luís 23
Campbell, John 30
care: attitude of carelessness 2–5; care as the feminization of human practices 65; care as the human ethos ix–xi, 11–13, 24–8, 55–6; case of the Tucunaré 72; challenging carelessness 5–8; concretisations of the way-of-being through care 93–115; examples of the way-of-being through care 120–41; fable-myth about care 21–2,

33–4, 69, 143; feng shui, the Chinese philosophy of care 138–41; golden rule 75–81; lack of care 119; negating care 117–18; pathological states of the way-of-being through care 116–19; philology of the word care 57–9; principles for the sustainability of Earth 93–5; resonances of essential care 72–92; ontological dimension of the human being 15, 56–7; right answers to carelessness 10–11
Chaplin, Charles 29
Che Guevara 82
Chuang-tsu 138
civilizational crisis 2–5; and the image of the human being 16–17; inadequate solutions to the crisis 5–8; the rise of a new paradigm 10–13; the rupture between the way-of-being through work and the way-of-being through care 64–6

Dalai Lama 30
Darwin, Charles 78
Dom Hélder Câmara 29
Duns Scotus 68
Dürer, Albrecht 87

176